MW01098927

WordPerfect® for Windows™ Hot Tips

Read Gilgen

WordPerfect for Windows Hot Tips

Copyright©1993 by Que® Corporation

All rights reserved. Printed in the United States of America. No part of this book may be used or reproduced in any form or by any means, or stored in a database or retrieval system, without prior written permission of the publisher except in the case of brief quotations embodied in critical articles and reviews. Making copies of any part of this book for any purpose other than your own personal use is a violation of United States copyright laws. For information, address Que Corporation, 11711 N. College Ave., Carmel, IN 46032.

Library of Congress Catalog No.: 92-84094

ISBN: 1-56529-175-1

This book is sold *as is*, without warranty of any kind, either express or implied, respecting the contents of this book, including but not limited to implied warranties for the book's quality, performance, merchantability, or fitness for any purpose. Neither Que Corporation nor its dealers or distributors shall be liable to the purchaser or any other person or entity with respect to any liability, loss, or damage caused or alleged to have been caused directly or indirectly by this book.

96   95   94   93   4   3   2   1

Interpretation of the printing code: the rightmost double-digit number is the year of the book's printing; the rightmost single-digit number, the number of the book's printing. For example, a printing code of 93-1 shows that the first printing of the book occurred in 1993.

All terms mentioned in this book that are known to be trademarks or service marks have been appropriately capitalized. Que cannot attest to the accuracy of this information. Use of a term in this book should not be regarded as affecting the validity of any trademark or service mark.

Windows is a trademark of Microsoft Corporation.

WordPerfect is a registered trademark and Button Bar is a trademark of WordPerfect Corporation.

Screen reproductions in this book were created using Collage Plus from Inner Media, Inc., Hollis, NH.

Dedication

To my father who taught me the difference between "lay" and "lie," and to my mother who taught me never to do either. To Sue, forever my companion, friend, and support.

Credits

Publisher
Lloyd J. Short

Associate Publisher
Rick Ranucci

Publishing Plan Manager
Thomas H. Bennett

Operations Manager
Sheila Cunningham

Book Designer
Scott Cook

Title Manager
Charles O. Stewart, III

Acquisitions Editor
Chris Katsaropoulos

Product Director
Steven M. Schafer

Production Editor
Heather Northrup

Editors
Elsa M. Bell
Jane A. Cramer
J. Christopher Nelson

Technical Editor
Mitch Milam

Production Team
Claudia Bell
Julie Brown
Paula Carroll
Laurie Casey
Michelle Cleary
Mark Enochs
Brook Farling
Howard Jones
Heather Kaufman
Bob LaRoche
Linda Seifert
Sandra Shay
Phil Worthington

Indexer
Joy Dean Lee

Composed in *Utopia* and *MCPdigital* by Que Corporation

About The Author

Read Gilgen is Director of Learning Support Services at the University of Wisconsin, Madison. He holds a doctorate in Latin American Literature. His professional interests include instructional media, microcomputers, and other technology in support of higher education, especially foreign language education. He has taught and written extensively on DOS and WordPerfect, and is a WordPerfect Certified Resource. He is a contributing author to Que's *Using WordPerfect for Windows 5.2, Special Edition.*

Table of Contents

Introduction

Whether you're a beginning or experienced WordPerfect for Windows user, the shortcuts and powerful techniques presented in *WordPerfect for Windows Hot Tips* will help improve your proficiency. In this book, you find information about the subtle program features you were too busy to read about in the documentation. You also find undocumented secrets, tips, and proven advice.

Unlike some computer books, it's not necessary to read the chapters or tips in this book in any particular order. Each chapter includes tips for a particular feature or function of WordPerfect for Windows.

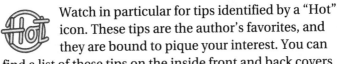 Watch in particular for tips identified by a "Hot" icon. These tips are the author's favorites, and they are bound to pique your interest. You can find a list of these tips on the inside front and back covers of this book.

If you want a comprehensive overview of WordPerfect for Windows, pick up a copy of Que's *Using WordPerfect for Windows 5.2*, Special Edition.

Book Conventions

Certain conventions are used in *WordPerfect for Windows Hot Tips* to help you understand the techniques and features described in the text. This section provides examples of these conventions.

Words printed in uppercase include DOS commands (CHKDSK) and file names (STATUS.DOC). The following table shows special formatting used in this book.

Format	Meaning
italics	Emphasized text and variables
boldface	Hot keys for menu options and words user types
`special typeface`	Direct quotations of words that appear on-screen or in a figure; menu command prompts

In most cases, keys are represented as they appear on the keyboard. The Print Screen key is abbreviated PrtSc, Page Up is PgUp, Insert is Ins, and so on; on your keyboard, these key names may be spelled out or abbreviated differently.

Throughout the text, the term *Enter* is used instead of *Return* for the Enter key.

Ctrl+F1 indicates that you press the Ctrl key and hold it down while you press the F1 key. Other key combinations (such as Alt+Esc) are performed in the same manner. If key combinations aren't indicated with a plus sign (+), don't hold down any of the keys; press each key once in the order listed (for example, End Home).

1

CHAPTER

Settling into the WordPerfect for Windows and Windows Interface

No matter what your background, if you are new to WordPerfect for Windows, you have plenty to learn about WordPerfect as well as about Windows' graphical interface. This chapter focuses on the kinds of things that make getting started or making the transition a bit easier. For example, when is it best to use a mouse? When should you use the keyboard? How can you take full advantage of the GUI? Does it really require less learning to become an expert WordPerfect user in the Windows environment? And finally, how can you set up WordPerfect for Windows for the fastest and most efficient performance?

Use the basic installation

The WordPerfect installation is designed to do a very good job of organizing your WordPerfect files when you select the basic installation. Unless you are sure that you need certain files in special or unusual locations, let Word-Perfect do the organizing work for you. Basic installation places files in the following locations:

Location	Files
C:\WPWIN	The main WordPerfect program files
C:\WPC	Files such as File Manager, Speller, Thesaurus, and Printer resource files that can run separately or that can be shared among other WordPerfect Corporation Windows applications
C:\WPWIN\MACROS	All macros, keyboards, and Button Bar files
C:\WPWIN\GRAPHICS	All graphics figures
C:\WPWIN\LEARN	All tutorial, learning files

Use the keyboard whenever possible

Using the keyboard is not inherently less intuitive than using a mouse; in fact, the keyboard is usually faster than the mouse once you learn the keystrokes. You can accomplish nearly everything in WordPerfect for Windows with the keyboard alone. Here are just a few of the keystrokes you can use in place of "mousing around":

Keystroke(s)	Mouse Equivalent
Alt+*letter*	Select from the main menu
Letter	Select from submenus
Tab	Move from one control to another while in a dialog box
Alt+space bar	Open the control menu for an application
Alt+hyphen	Open the control menu for a document

WordPerfect assigns certain functions to function keys, such as Ctrl+F4 to close an open document. In addition, you can access many functions by using mnemonic keystrokes. For example, you can press Alt+F(file), S(save) to save a file.

Name search in lists

List boxes often are used for selecting a file or some other listed feature. Although you can use the mouse to point and click, or to scroll through the list, often you can locate and select the item more quickly by typing the first few characters of its name. For example, press F4 to display the Open File dialog box. Tab to the files list or click it with a mouse. Type **t** and the cursor moves to the first file in the list that begins with t. Continue typing the name or move the cursor with the arrow keys to the item you want. Press Enter to select the item.

Use the mouse if your hand is already on it

In many cases, using the mouse is not only natural, but also more efficient than using the keyboard to accomplish the same task. For example, you can use the mouse to direct the editing I-beam pointer to where you want to edit your text and click the left (primary) mouse button to reposition the insertion point.

In other cases, moving your hand from the mouse to the keyboard makes less sense than moving the mouse and selecting a button. For example, if your hand already is on the mouse after having selected a command such as Close, moving the mouse to the Yes, No, or Cancel buttons is probably quicker than moving your hand to the keyboard and typing the appropriate hot key (**Y**, **N**, or **Enter**).

Double-click the mouse to select more quickly

If you are using the mouse to make a selection from a list, you generally can double-click to select the item and to perform the procedure. For example, if you select a file from the list in the Open File dialog box, you can double-click on a file name to both select and open the file.

Use the scroll bar to scroll through your document

The vertical scroll bar at the right side of the screen helps you move quickly from one part of your document to another. The scroll box (the plain box between the two arrow boxes) tells you roughly where you are relative to the rest of your text. Position the mouse pointer on the scroll box, hold down the primary (left) mouse button, and move the scroll box up or down; the text scrolls accordingly.

Remember that the scroll bar does not move the insertion point

Although the text scrolls up or down when you use the scroll bar, the insertion point does not move. Two problems can occur:

- If you move a direction key (for example, the left or right arrow key), the display returns to the insertion point.

- If you attempt to apply a formatting feature (for example, margin settings), the code for that feature is placed relative to the insertion point (which has not moved), instead of in the screen you have scrolled to.

To avoid reverting back to the original screen location, click the mouse on the current screen to change the insertion point.

Learn the CUA keystrokes

 CUA stands for *Common User Access* and refers to a set of keystrokes that are used in all Windows applications. If you are arriving at WordPerfect for Windows after having used the DOS version of WordPerfect, the CUA keyboard layout feels rather strange and can be difficult to get used to. If, however, you're already used to Windows-based applications, WordPerfect for Windows' CUA keystrokes seem natural and easy.

The CUA interface has three basic, and somewhat different, parts. One of the more important of the three is the way that cursor control keys work. These keys, and their functions, include the following:

Key(s)	Function
Home	Moves cursor to the left of a line
End	Moves cursor to the end of a line
Ctrl+Home	Moves to the beginning of a document
Ctrl+End	Moves to the end of a document

Another use of the CUA keyboard is for editing controls. These keys include the following:

Key(s)	Function
Shift+Del	Cuts a selected block of text
Ctrl+X	Cuts a selected block of text
Shift+Insert	Pastes a block of text
Ctrl+V	Pastes a block of text
Ctrl+Insert	Copies a selected block of text
Ctrl+C	Copies a selected block of text

The third is the use of function keys for common tasks. Note, however, that Windows reserves relatively few function keys for itself; application developers, such as WordPerfect Corporation, assign most function keys as the developers need them.

Key(s)	Function
F1	Help
ESC	Cancel, Escape
F4	Open
Ctrl+F4	Close document
Alt+F4	Close application

The preceding keystrokes are standard on nearly every Windows application, so moving from one application to another is easier because you don't have to learn a whole new set of keystrokes. In the long run, learning this new approach is worth the effort.

Minimize rather than exit WordPerfect to save time

Because WordPerfect takes several seconds to start up, learn to minimize WordPerfect or use the Task List to change to another Windows application. To minimize WordPerfect for Windows, click the single down arrow button at the upper right corner of the screen (see figure 1.1). You also can press Alt+Space to display the Application Control menu and select Minimize. These procedures minimize *any* Windows program.

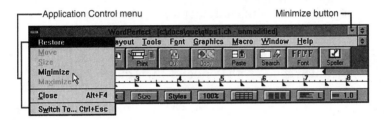

Fig. 1.1 *Minimizing WordPerfect.*

Double-clicking the WordPerfect for Windows icon or selecting WordPerfect for Windows from the Task List (press Ctrl+Esc, select WordPerfect from the list, and press Enter or select Switch To) returns you quickly to whatever you were doing before you changed applications.

Use shortcuts for exiting WordPerfect

When you are finished with WordPerfect, you can exit it by selecting File, Exit(Alt+F4). If you use the mouse, the quickest way to exit is to double-click the Application Control menu icon in the upper left corner of the screen instead of pulling down the File menu to select Exit.

Speed up Windows

One of the most common complaints about Windows programs, including WordPerfect for Windows, is that they are much slower than their DOS counterparts. You can, however, do several things to increase the speed and efficiency of WordPerfect for Windows:

- Edit your CONFIG.SYS file to contain the following line: FILES=60. Be sure to save your CONFIG.SYS file as ASCII (DOS) text or you won't be able to start your computer correctly.

- Make sure your computer has sufficient memory (RAM). You need at least 4M, but 8M is better.

- Use some sort of disk-caching program. SMARTDRV, which comes with Windows 3.1, is quite suitable, although some third-party programs such as Super PC-Kwik are even better. The Windows 3.0 version of SMARTDRV is not very good at all.

- If you run Windows in 386-Enhanced Mode, create a permanent swap file on your hard disk of at least 5M. Because the procedures differ for Windows 3.0 and Windows 3.1, see your Windows reference for instructions on this relatively simple procedure.

- If you are running Windows in Super VGA mode, try running it at standard VGA resolution, 16-colors instead. Windows has to work harder at higher resolutions, which, with some graphics boards, slows everything down.

And finally, if you are using Windows 3.0, consider upgrading to Windows 3.1. In addition to some slight improvements in speed, you also achieve much greater system stability.

Edit CONFIG.SYS or AUTOEXEC.BAT in WordPerfect

If you need to edit any ASCII or DOS text file, such as CONFIG.SYS, AUTOEXEC.BAT, or WIN.INI, you can do so in WordPerfect. However, you must take a few precautions so that the changed files still work.

Open your AUTOEXEC.BAT file, for example, as you would any other file in WordPerfect for Windows. WordPerfect displays the Convert File dialog box. Select OK to open the file in WordPerfect. After making the modifications to the file, select File, Save As and make sure that ASCII Generic WordProcessor (DOS) is selected in the Format field before choosing OK. If any of the lines of your file are so long that they wrap back to the left margin, you must save the file in this format for the file to work properly.

Change preferences to suit your tastes

If you don't like a particular WordPerfect default setting, chances are you can change it to match your own preferences. For example, by default, WordPerfect documents are formatted for Full Justification (both left and right margins). Using the Initial Codes option under File, Preferences, you can change the default to Left Justification.

Until you become familiar with the program and the way it works, however, you should not make many preference changes. Most default settings have been determined based on customer feedback over many years.

Customize WordPerfect's startup options

You can alter the way WordPerfect starts up by adding a startup option to the program's properties. From the Windows Program Manager, click the WordPerfect program icon, select File, Properties (Alt+Enter), and then add one or more of the following to the end of the Command Line in the Program Item Properties dialog box:

Item	Action
filename	Starts WordPerfect with the named file already open. Be sure to include the full path name if the file is not in your default document directory.
/x	Overrides any changes you have made to your preferences and returns to WordPerfect's original default settings.
/m-macroname	Starts up WordPerfect and immediately executes the named macro.
/d-drive\directory	Enables you to specify where WordPerfect stores its temporary and overflow files.

Check the date of your copy of WordPerfect

Although many months may pass between official upgrades of WordPerfect, the company often releases interim versions that correct certain problems, but that also sometimes include new or enhanced features. Publications that deal with WordPerfect often refer to release dates rather than version numbers.

To verify the date of your copy of WordPerfect, select Help, About WordPerfect. Your license number, which you can edit, also appears in the About WordPerfect dialog box.

Share files between WordPerfect for Windows and WordPerfect for DOS

If you have been using WordPerfect for DOS, you will find that many of the files used in WordPerfect for Windows are exactly the same as those used by WordPerfect for DOS. These files include the Speller and the Thesaurus data files, the printer definition files, and several utility files. After you install WordPerfect for Windows, start up your DOS version of WordPerfect, go to Setup (Shift+F1), Location of files, and make the following changes (if you customized your WordPerfect for Windows installation, change the settings according to your actual location of files):

C:\WPC	Thesaurus/Speller/ Hyphenation main and supplementary dictionaries; Printer files
C:\WPWIN	Style files and LIBRARY.STY
C:\WPWIN\GRAPHICS	Graphic files

If you plan to continue using both WordPerfect for DOS and WordPerfect for Windows (a good idea at least for a while), you can remove duplicate or older versions of files that both programs now share. From your C:\WP51 directory, you can delete PTR.EXE, PTR.HLP, GRAPHCNV.EXE, SPELL.EXE, WP.DRS, WP{WP}US.LEX, and WP{WP}US.THS.

Use your WordPerfect for DOS customized spelling dictionary

If you have been using WordPerfect for DOS for some time, you may have customized your spelling dictionary, added words to your supplementary dictionary, or even customized your hyphenation dictionary. If so, you should copy the following files to the C:\WPC directory: WP{WP}US.LEX, WP{WP}US.SUP, WP{WP}US.HYC, and WP{WP}US.SPW. If you are short on hard disk space, you can delete these files from C:\WP51 because both the Windows and the DOS versions of WordPerfect now share them in the C:\WPC directory.

2

CHAPTER

Entering Text

Although most people often think of word processing in terms of correcting and editing, a large percentage of a word processing operator's time is spent trying to type the correct characters, words, and phrases. The tips found in this chapter relate primarily to basic text entry (typing) tasks. In this chapter, beginners learn how to do things right from the start. This chapter, however, is also for seasoned veterans who can learn many time-saving procedures. If followed, these tips not only help you to enter data, but also simplify the task of correcting and formatting your text later.

Hide the Ruler and Button Bars for more workspace

You want to have as much screen space as possible in order to see the "big picture" as you enter your text. To gain more room, hide both the Button Bar and the Ruler. Remember that formatting is relatively unimportant during basic text entry because you can apply margins, fonts, and special formatting effects later.

To hide the ruler, select View, **R**uler (Alt+Shift+F3). Repeat this procedure to display the Ruler.

To hide the Button Bar, select View, Button Bar. You also can hide the Button Bar by clicking it with the secondary (right) mouse button and then choosing Hide. Select View, Button Bar to display the Button Bar.

Save your work early and often

Often the most valuable tip is also the simplest: *Save your work early and often.* Sometimes you may think you don't yet have enough text to make saving your work in progress worth the effort. But quantity is only part of the consideration. The creativity expended in writing even one paragraph is difficult to replicate.

Use shortcuts and buttons instead of menus

You usually don't learn two complete sets of procedures; instead, you become comfortable with one. Make sure you learn and use procedures that save you time. Using menus to access a WordPerfect feature may take several keystrokes or mouse clicks, whereas a single button or quick keystroke can get the job done quickly. Use the method that makes sense. If your hand is already resting on the mouse, use the Button Bar. If your hand is on the keyboard, use the function key.

Open several documents at once

WordPerfect allows you to work on up to nine documents at a time—a feature that can be a great help when you are working on several projects. For example, you can prepare an outline in document one, open another for the text, and have still another for the bibliographic references. You can easily copy text from one document and paste it into one of the other eight documents.

To switch quickly from one document to another, select Window and choose from among the open documents listed. You also can cycle through your open documents by pressing Ctrl+F6 (Next Document) or Shift+Ctrl+F6 (Previous Document).

Use Draft Mode to work more quickly

Because WordPerfect for Windows displays a graphical representation of what you create, the computer has to work harder to process what you type than it does for a DOS-based, text-only word processor. If you are working on a slower computer and your typing seems to lag behind, try working in Draft Mode by choosing View, Draft.

Use a monospaced font for basic text creation

If you prefer working in the regular graphic mode, you want your text to be as large as possible, but you also want to be able to see an entire line of text without having to scroll to the right or left.

One way to keep your text visible is to use a standard monospaced font, such as Courier (10 pitch, or 12 point) as your Document Initial Font. You can change the Document Initial Font when you are ready to format your document by choosing Layout, Document, Initial Font.

Note: If your document is heavily formatted (for example, tabular columns), work with the font you intend to use for your fixed output.

Use Zoom to view the full width of your text

One way to view the full width of your text, regardless of your font size, is to use WordPerfect's Zoom feature. This feature enables you to size your text to fit within your display area without changing the actual size of the printed text.

Select View, Zoom and first try selecting To Page Width. If the text is still too small or large, then try selecting Other and specifying the exact percentage of the display. For example, Courier at Super VGA proportions (800x600) might look best at 115% of normal size, but Courier at standard VGA (640x480) might be best at 100% of normal size.

When you find a Zoom size that works best for you for the font you most often use, consider changing the default size by selecting File, Preferences, Display, Zoom and setting the size you decide upon.

Do not use spaces to line up text

You can change the format for nearly anything you type in WordPerfect after you type it; however, if you use certain formatting procedures as you create your text, subsequent editing and formatting is much easier. Don't worry about page breaks, fonts, or even margins and columns, but make sure that you use tabs, indents, centering, flush right, and hard returns correctly.

Always use tabs to align your text, especially with tabular columns of data. Using spaces to align text may look correct on-screen (especially if used in draft mode or with a monospaced font, such as Courier or Letter Gothic), but if you change to a proportionally spaced font, such as Times Roman, the formatting falls to pieces. Tabs always advance to the correct position, regardless of the font you use.

Likewise, always use Center (Shift+F7) or Flush Right (Alt+F7) to center or right align your text. Using spaces to align your text results in formatting disaster when you change fonts or margins. Pressing Shift+F7 or Alt+F7 is also much quicker and easier than creating the spaces necessary to center or right align text.

Use Indent to set a temporary left margin

One of the most important format codes you should learn is the Indent code, used to set a temporary left margin. Consider the paragraph in figure 2.1:

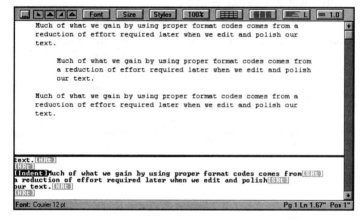

Fig. 2.1 *An indented paragraph.*

The brute force method of indenting a paragraph consists of pressing Tab, typing the first line, pressing Enter, pressing Tab, typing the second line, pressing Enter, and so on. Any additions, deletions, or font changes made to the paragraph result in a real mess.

The proper way to format such a paragraph is to use an Indent code to set a temporary left margin. Press Indent (F7), or select Layout, Paragraph, Indent to insert the code, then type the text of the paragraph. Do not press Enter until you finish the entire paragraph. When you do press Enter, the insertion point returns to the original left margin.

Note: An indent code placed at any tab stop sets a temporary left margin at that point. For example, if you press Indent at the 4" tab stop, your entire paragraph is indented to the 4" mark.

To indent both the left and right sides of a paragraph equally, insert a Double Indent code by selecting Layout, Paragraph, Double Indent (Ctrl+Shift+F7).

Leave your paragraph hanging with a hanging indent

To create a hanging paragraph, select Layout, Paragraph, Hanging Indent(Ctrl+F7). Then type your paragraph as you normally do. When you finish typing, press Enter to return to the left margin. Figure 2.2 gives an example of a hanging paragraph.

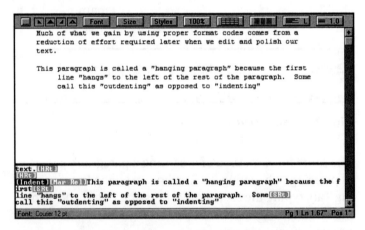

Fig. 2.2 *A hanging paragraph.*

Use shortcuts for bold and other attributes

Certain textual attributes, such as **bold**, <u>underline</u>, and *italic* are used to highlight or emphasize your text. As a matter of good form, italics are a gentle way to emphasize something to your readers; bold fairly shouts at them. As a general rule, avoid underlining unless your printer cannot print italics.

Although you can add these attributes later, you will find it more natural to add them at the same time you originally create your text. WordPerfect has shortcut keys for these attributes:

Bold	Ctrl+B
Italic	Ctrl+I
Underline	Ctrl+U

Insert commonly used phrases into your text with the Glossary

If you do a lot of typing, you may repeatedly type many phrases, for example, your name, your company name, the title of a certain reference work, an address, or certain standard phrases such as ASAP (as soon as possible).

WordPerfect's Glossary feature can help. To add a phrase to the Glossary, play the macro GLOSEDIT and type the abbreviation in the Abbreviation text box and the full text in the Full Text text box. The full text can include very long phrases and multiple lines separated by hard returns as well as WordPerfect characters. However, you cannot use attributes, such as bold or italic, or other formatting codes, and you are limited to 256 characters. Press OK to save the new Glossary entry.

Then, to use your new entry, simply type the abbreviation into your document and play the GLOSSARY macro. The abbreviation is replaced by the full text you specified.

You may want to add the GLOSSARY macro to your favorite Button Bar or assign it to a Ctrl+key combination. (See Chapter 4, "Getting Started with Macros," for more information and other helpful macro shortcuts.)

Use WordPerfect's 1500 special characters

In addition to all the characters and numbers you find on your keyboard, WordPerfect provides several hundred characters and symbols. The WordPerfect reference manual lists in Appendix A some 1500 characters including foreign language characters, scientific characters, and typographic symbols.

Note: Because WordPerfect graphically creates these additional characters, your printer must support graphics. Also, some of the character sets have certain restrictions or qualifications. Consult the WordPerfect manual's Appendix A for more information.

To access any of the WordPerfect characters, press Ctrl+W, or select Font, WP Characters. The WordPerfect Characters dialog box displays the ASCII character set, the first of 12 character sets. You can select the character Set you want, find the Character you want, and then if you want to leave the dialog box open so you can select additional characters, choose Insert. Select Insert and Close to insert the character and close the dialog box at the same time.

If you know the character set and character number you want, simply type in the Number text box the number of the character set followed by a comma and the number of the character. For example, to select the paragraph symbol (¶), you type **4,5**. Press Enter and WordPerfect inserts the character in your text.

Compose special characters on-the-fly

Suppose you want to impress your client, Mr. Gómez, by showing that you know his name carries an accent on the o. Type **Mr. G**, and then press Ctrl+W. Rather than browsing to find the ´ in the Number text box, type o followed by the apostrophe (') and press Enter. WordPerfect is smart enough to know that those two characters mean you want to compose the special character ´ .

You can use many combinations of characters to more quickly select the special character you want. Among these are the following:

WordPerfect Character	Char Set, Char Number	Shortcut Keys
½	4,17	/2
.	4,3	*.
•	4,0	**
o	4,1	*o
—	4,34	m-
©	4,23	co
™	4,41	tm
¢	4,19	c/
´	1,27	'
`	1,47	'
ü	1,71	u"
¥	4,12	Y=
ç	1,39	c,

Follow the above patterns for other foreign language and special characters. If you can't find a shortcut key combination, you still can use the character set numbers, or browse the WordPerfect Characters dialog box.

Use fancy bullets to dress up your paragraphs

By using special WordPerfect characters, you can call attention to lists of items or important paragraphs. For example, to create a pointing hand bullet, press Ctrl+W, type **5,21** in the Number text box, and choose Insert and Close.

 The hand (5,21) makes a fancy bullet.

Make bullets quickly

WordPerfect has two bullet macros. BULLETDF.WCM lets you specify the bullet character you want to use for your bulleted paragraphs, and BULLET.WCM automatically adds bullets to your text. Both of these macros are on the FEATURES Button Bar.

Run the BULLETDF macro to define what bullet the BULLET macro uses. You can select the Standard Bullet Character or any Other Character(s) you choose. If you use Other Characters, you can use any of the WP Characters by pressing Ctrl+W while in the Other Characters text box. Choose OK to save your bullet choice.

Wherever you want a bullet in your document, run the BULLET macro. Whatever characters you specified with BULLETDF are inserted at the beginning of the current paragraph along with an Indent code.

To add bullets and to indent several paragraphs at once, select the paragraphs before running the BULLET macro.

Use typographically correct quote marks

When creating typographically correct documents, you want to use the proper opening and closing quote mark pairs ("") rather than the generic " character. Instead of using the WordPerfect Characters dialog box to insert these quote mark pairs, you can use WordPerfect's Smart Quotes feature to select and display the proper quote mark.

You play a macro to activate the Smart Quotes feature. Select Macro, Play (Alt+F10) and enter SMQUOTE. Word-Perfect displays a menu that lets you turn on, turn off, or configure your Smart Quotes. If you turn on the feature, each time you type a quote mark, WordPerfect checks to see whether a space precedes the quote. If so, WordPerfect types the opening quote, character 4,32 ("). If the character preceding the quote is a character, Word-Perfect types the closing quote, character 4,31 ("). Typing the quote mark a second time changes the opening quote to a closing one, and vice versa. The same applies to single quote marks.

If you choose to configure Smart Quotes, WordPerfect displays the Smart-Quoter Options dialog box (see fig. 2.3). Here you can change the characters used for the quote, enable Smart Quotes upon starting up WordPerfect, have WordPerfect alert you when Smart Quotes is activated, and even specify that regular inch marks (") be used with numbers.

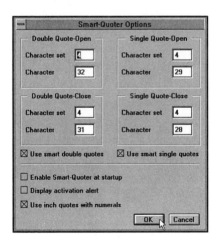

Fig. 2.3   *The Smart-Quoter Options dialog box.*

Caution: If you must export your text to an ASCII file or to some other word processing program, the special quotes probably will be lost. If you know you are going to be exporting your text, stick to the standard (") quote marks, or first use Replace to substitute regular quote marks for your smart quotes.

3

Editing Documents

Unless you are very unlike the rest of us, you won't create a perfect document the first time you type it. This chapter is all about changing your text, from the simple corrections of typographical errors to more complex rearrangement and revision.

All WordPerfect users should try to reduce, as far as possible, the number of keystrokes (or mouse clicks) needed to accomplish a certain task. As you read the procedures in this book, always ask yourself whether this procedure is more efficient than the method you now use. If the answer is an honest no, stick with what you're doing. But if the answer is yes or maybe, then you owe it to yourself to try the new procedure.

Open Reveal Codes using the mouse

If you are using the mouse, an easy way to open, or close, the Reveal Codes window is to move the mouse pointer to the small black bar above or below the right scroll bar. When the pointer turns to a double arrow, click and drag the bar up or down to open and size the Reveal Codes window (see figure 3.1).

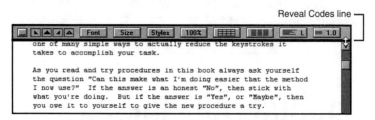

Reveal Codes line

Fig. 3.1   *Using the mouse to open the Reveal Codes window.*

To close the Reveal Codes window with the mouse, position the mouse pointer on the Reveal Codes dividing line (the pointer again turns into a double arrow), and drag the line all the way to the top or bottom of the screen.

Learn quick keyboard cursor movement

Most keyboards these days come with separate cursor control keys and numeric keypad. Note, however, that a duplicate set of cursor control keys are found on the numeric keypad. If you press Num Lock (the Num Lock light should be off), the numeric keypad keys work the same as the gray ones in the separate cursor key section.

For most keyboard controlled movement of the insertion point, the keys on the numeric keypad are easier to use and more efficient. The numeric keypad enables you to reach the arrow keys and Home, End, and so on by moving just your fingers and not your whole arm and hand.

Learn even quicker keyboard cursor movement

Moving the insertion point is a breeze with the mouse, but when you're busy typing, having to move your hand to the mouse can slow you down and break your concentration. Instead, learn to use these handy keystrokes that move the insertion point rapidly.

Keystroke	Moves the insertion point
Ctrl+Right Arrow	One word to the right
Ctrl+Left Arrow	One word to the left
Ctrl+Up Arrow	To the preceding paragraph
Ctrl+Down Arrow	To the following paragraph
Page Up (PgUp)	To the preceding screen
Page Down (PgDn)	To the following screen
Alt+PgUp	To the preceding page
Alt+PgDn	To the following page
Ctrl+PgUp	A screen to the right
Ctrl+PgDn	A screen to the left

Go all the way to the top of the document

Pressing Ctrl+Home takes you to the top of your WordPerfect document; however, the insertion point doesn't really go all the way to the top. Instead, it positions itself immediately *following* any formatting codes found at the beginning of the document. To position the insertion point at the absolute top, press Ctrl+Home twice.

Correct mistaken cursor movements

If you ever accidentally press one or a combination of keys that causes the insertion point to end up far away from what you were working on, you can find your place easily because WordPerfect remembers the last location of your insertion point. To return to your last insertion point position, select Edit, Go To(Ctrl+G), and then select Last Position.

Caution: If you move your insertion point before trying to return to the last position, WordPerfect "forgets" that location and cannot take you back.

Quickly delete whole words

To delete a word at a time, position the insertion point on the word you want to delete and press Ctrl+Backspace. If you have several words to delete, keep pressing Ctrl+Backspace. This action deletes the word and any punctuation up to the next word. However, this action does not keep deleting past the paragraph boundary.

Quickly delete to the end of the line

To delete from the position of the insertion point to the end of the line, press Ctrl+Del. For example, you want to change the name in the following:

> TO: George Reynolds Hornblower, Esq.

Position the insertion point to the left of George and press Ctrl+Del to remove the rest of the line. Now you can type the new name.

Quickly delete whole sections of text

You can use the mouse to get rid of whole large sections of text. Position the mouse pointer at the beginning of the section you want to delete. Click and drag the mouse to the end of the section, and then press Backspace or Delete.

Quickly replace old text with new text

If you just want to replace selected text with something new, you don't need to delete the text first. After selecting the text, start typing the new material and the selected text disappears.

Use Undelete to restore mistakenly deleted text

WordPerfect remembers the last *three* things you deleted and lets you restore any of them. Position the insertion point where you want to restore the deleted text and select Edit, Undelete (Alt+Shift+Backspace). Your most recent deletion appears. From the Undelete dialog box, choose Previous or Next to cycle through the three available deletions. When you see the text you want to restore, select Restore.

Caution: You probably don't realize how often you delete things by pressing the Backspace key. If you need to restore something that you deleted, do so soon before you are unable to recover it.

Use Delete and Undelete for "quick and dirty" cutting and pasting

Delete the text and codes you want to move, move to where you want the text and codes, and use Edit, Undelete (Alt+Shift+Backspace) to restore the text to the new location.

Caution: Using Delete/Undelete to move text or codes can be a bit dangerous because if you don't immediately move and restore the deleted text, you may lose it.

Shift-click to Select text quickly

Although you can drag the mouse to select text, you also can select text by using the mouse to place the insertion point at one end of the block, holding down the Shift key, and then using the mouse to position the insertion point at the other end of the block. WordPerfect then selects all the text between these two points.

Use Shift plus direction keys to select text

There are two disadvantages to selecting text with the mouse: your hands have to leave the keyboard in search of the mouse, and dragging isn't always very precise.

A simple method for selecting text is to hold down the Shift key, and then use the cursor movement keys (the direction arrows, Home, End, etc.) to extend the end of the block of selected text.

Use the Select key to select specific text

The Select key (F8) makes selecting specific segments of text even easier. When you press F8, Select Mode appears at the lower left on the status bar. With Select Mode turned on, the insertion point then advances to the next character you type.

For example, if you press F8 and then press the space bar, the selected block extends one word, including the space that follows it. Press the space bar several times to select several words. Likewise, if you press the period, the insertion point advances to the end of the sentence (if the sentence ends with a period). You can even use Ctrl+W to extend the Select block to a special WordPerfect character. Finally, to quickly and accurately select a paragraph at a time, press Select (F8) and press Enter.

Click more than once to select text elements

If your hand already is resting on the mouse, using the mouse to select text makes sense. A quicker and possibly more precise way than dragging to select a single word is to double-click the word. WordPerfect highlights (selects) the entire word and the space following it.

If you triple-click, you select an entire sentence. Clicking four times selects the whole paragraph, including any extra hard returns up to the text of the next paragraph.

Use the keyboard to adjust a mouse selection

If you have selected text with the mouse, but need to make a minor adjustment in the block that has been selected, hold down the Shift key and move the cursor to the desired end of the block.

Learn shortcut keys for cutting and pasting

Another of word processing's essential tasks is cutting or copying text and moving it to another location. In addition to the regular menus (Edit and then Cut, Copy, or Paste), you can use two other sets of keystrokes to help you speed this operation:

Action	Menu	WPWin Shortcut	Windows Shortcut
Cut	Edit, Cut	Shift+Delete	Ctrl+X
Copy	Edit, Copy	Ctrl+Insert	Ctrl+C
Paste	Edit, Paste	Shift+Insert	Ctrl+V

All of these keystrokes are standard Windows methods for cutting, copying, and pasting text. Find the method that you can remember and use most efficiently and then learn it well, because you can use it in most other Windows programs as well.

Use the mouse to Drag and Drop

Perhaps the fastest method for moving text is Word-Perfect's Drag and Drop feature. If you select text with the mouse (or keyboard), you can move or copy text very quickly over short distances without returning to the keyboard.

Position the mouse pointer over the selected text (the I-beam pointer changes to an arrow). Hold down the primary (left) mouse button, and an icon showing a piece of paper being moved is added to the arrow (see figure 3.2). While holding down the mouse button, drag the pointer to where you want to paste the text. Watch the insertion point to determine exactly where the text will be inserted. Release the mouse button and your text is "dropped" into its new location.

You can copy text in the same manner. Follow the same steps for moving, but also hold down the Ctrl key. The Drag and Drop icon changes to a solid black background. When you release the mouse button, WordPerfect pastes a copy of the selected text in the new location, while the original copy remains in its original place.

Move hidden codes along with text

When you move a selected block of text, you must consider the codes that go along with the text. Format and font codes, if part of the selected text, also move with that text. Pairs of attribute codes, such as **bold** or *italics*, move along with the text only if they are both located entirely within the selected text. Use Reveal Codes to select exactly what you want.

If you do move a hidden format code and don't want the code at the new location, delete it or cut it and paste it back at the original location.

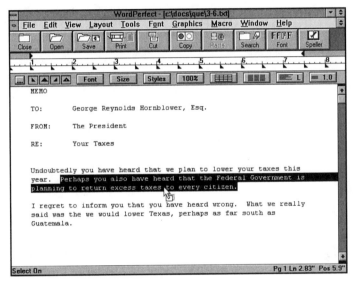

Fig. 3.2 *Moving text using Drag and Drop.*

Select text with attributes

If you select only part of some text that has been changed with a size or attribute code, the code remains for the text left behind and replicates itself for the text that is moved. For example, consider the following text:

The **very large bold** dog barked at my door.

If you select just the word "large" but leave the rest, "very bold" remains large and bold, and "large" remains both large and bold in its new location:

The **very bold** dog barked at my **large** door.

4

Getting Started with Macros

In this chapter, you find out about recording and using simple macros and using some of WordPerfect's pre-defined macros.

Try recording a macro

Sometimes, you only need to try a feature once to find out that it's easy and useful. If you've never created a macro, why not try it? The basic steps for recording any macro are as follows:

1. Choose **Macro**, **Record** (Ctrl+F10).

2. In the Macro Record dialog box, type the name of your macro with an optional Descriptive Name.

3. Choose **Record**.

4. Type the keystrokes and use the menu commands you normally use to accomplish the task at hand. Use the keyboard, not the mouse, for any editing. Everything that you type or do is recorded in the macro.

5. When you are finished, choose **Macro**, **Stop** (Ctrl+Shift+F10).

Close the document you used to create the macro (Ctrl+F4), and open a new document (Shift+F4).

To play a macro, choose **Macro**, **Play** (Alt+F10). Type the name of the macro and press Enter to select **Play**.

Assign macros to Ctrl+key combinations for quicker access

In some cases, the number of keystrokes required to play a macro nearly defeats the purpose of using a macro. You can play macros more quickly by assigning your macros to Ctrl+key combinations. When you assign a name to your macro, type **CTRL** and the other key you want to use (**CTRLA**, for example) in the Filename text box or press the Ctrl+key combination and WordPerfect inserts the name for you. You can assign macros to single digit numbers (CTRL9, for example) as well as to the letters *A-Z*.

Now instead of having to first choose **Macro**, **Play** and then enter a macro name, you simply press the Ctrl+key combination to play the macro.

Do not use reserved Ctrl+key combinations for macros

Certain Ctrl+key combinations already may be assigned to your keyboard, for example, Ctrl+P for printing. Although WordPerfect lets you record a CTRLP macro, pressing Ctrl+P to play it results instead in the action assigned to the keyboard (in this case, printing your document). To check whether the Ctrl+key combination is assigned, open a new blank document (File, New or Shift+F4) and then press the Ctrl+key combination. If you get an error message saying that CTRL*x*.WCM is not found, you can safely create a macro using that Ctrl+key name.

Following is a list of Ctrl+key combinations assigned to the CUA keyboard:

Ctrl+Key	Assigned Purpose
Ctrl+B	Bold
Ctrl+C	Copy
Ctrl+D	Line Draw
Ctrl+F	Full Justify
Ctrl+G	Go To
Ctrl+I	Italics
Ctrl+J	Center Justify
Ctrl+L	Left Justify
Ctrl+M	Macro Command Inserter
Ctrl+N	Font Normal
Ctrl+P	Print Full Document
Ctrl+R	Right Justify
Ctrl+S	Font Size
Ctrl+U	Underline
Ctrl+V	Paste
Ctrl+W	WordPerfect Characters
Ctrl+X	Cut
Ctrl+Z	Undo

Use WordPerfect's predefined macros

WordPerfect provides several predefined macros that range in power and functionality from relatively simple tasks to complex programs. The following list briefly defines these macros:

Note: The list of included macros varies depending upon release date. Check **Help, Using** Macros for a list of current shipping macros.

Macro name	Description
ADD	Adds pairs of attributes where other attributes already exist
BARCODE	Creates PostNet bar codes
BULLET	Adds bullets to paragraphs
BULLETDF	Defines the default bullet used with BULLET
CAPITAL	Capitalizes first letter of word
CODES	Prints codes that normally don't print (i.e. Reveal Codes, etc)
DELETE	Deletes a line
EDIT	Edits existing codes easily
ENDFOOT	Converts all endnotes to footnotes
ENVELOPE	Captures an address and prints it to an envelope
FIND	Searches for and deletes a bookmark created with FIND
FOOTEND	Converts all footnotes to endnotes
GLOSEDIT	Adds abbreviated words to glossary (used by GLOSSARY)
GLOSSARY	Expands glossary words
INLINE	Creates equations in a line of text
INSERT	Inserts a blank line
JUSTIFY	Sets line justification
LABELS	Sets up labels paper size definition based on commercially available labels
LINENUM	Goes to a specified line number in a macro

Macro name	Description
MARK	Sets a bookmark
MEMO	Creates a memo, letter, fax cover sheet, or itinerary
PAPER	Selects a paper size
PATHFILE	Inserts the document name and path at the cursor location
PLEADING	Sets pleading style defined by user
QFINDEX	Starts the Quick Finder File Indexer program
RECALC	Recalculates all formulas in a table
REPLACE	Searches and replaces codes such as fonts
SMQUOTE	Inserts typeset-quality quote marks
TABSET	Creates a tab setting
TRANSPOS	Switches the order of two characters

Assign Ctrl+key names to predefined macros

Predefined macros that accomplish simple tasks, such as CAPITAL, DELETE, and TRANSPOS, do not justify performing all the keystrokes required to type their full names. Instead, copy or convert these macros to Ctrl+key combinations. For example, to play the TRANSPOS macro by pressing Ctrl+T, follow these steps:

1. Select Macro, Play (Alt+F10). The Play Macro dialog box appears.

2. From the list of macro files, select (but do not play) TRANSPOS.WCM.

3. Select Options, and press the space bar or hold down the primary (left) mouse button to view the pop-up list.

4. Select Copy. WordPerfect displays the Copy File dialog box (see fig. 4.1).

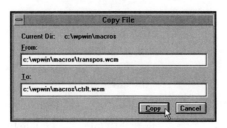

Fig. 4.1 *Copying a macro using the Copy File dialog box.*

5. In the To text box, type the new file name for the macro (for example, \ctrlt.wcm) and select Copy.

6. Select Cancel to close the Play Macro dialog box.

You now can play the TRANSPOS macro by pressing Ctrl+T.

Assign macros to the Macro menu

Another way to keep your favorite macros at hand is to assign them to the Macro menu. You can select macros from the Macro menu with the mouse, or you can access them by typing just a couple of keystrokes (for example, Alt+M, 1). Suppose that you want to assign the GLOSEDIT macro to the Macro menu. Follow these steps:

1. Select Macro, Assign to Menu. WordPerfect displays the Assign Macro to Menu dialog box (see fig. 4.2).

2. To add a macro to the end of the list, press the down arrow key until the black cursor bar is at the list's end. Adding macros to the end of the list prevents you from having to rememorize the numbers of the other assigned macros (although you can list macros in any order you decide).

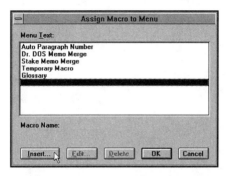

Fig. 4.2 *The Assign Macro to Menu dialog box.*

3. Select Insert to display the Insert Macro Menu Item dialog box.

4. In the Macro Name text box, type the name of the macro you want to add.

5. Type a descriptive macro name in the Menu Text text box.

6. Select OK to close the Insert Macro Menu Item dialog box, and then select OK again to close the Assign Macro to Menu dialog box.

To use the macro you just assigned to the Macro Menu, select Macro, and then the number (1-9) next to the macro you want to use. Remember that you can assign only nine macros to the Macro menu; make sure they are your nine most important ones.

5

The Button Bar

The WordPerfect for Windows Button Bar is a quick way to access WordPerfect features and procedures. When you are delving deep into a menu to access a certain often used feature, or when no quick keyboard alternative exists for a feature, see whether there is a button that can help you. If not, you can add buttons to your own customized Button Bars.

Leave the Button Bar on

Except when you are typing long documents and want more screen space, leave your Button Bar active.

To activate a Button Bar, select View, **B**utton Bar. The Button Bar remains active even if you open other documents or exit and return to WordPerfect. If you exit WordPerfect with a Button Bar active, that same Button Bar remains active when you start WordPerfect the next time.

Use WordPerfect's predefined Button Bars

In addition to the default, basic Button Bar, WordPerfect provides 10 Button Bars that help with specific editing or formatting tasks. These include the following:

Name	Buttons/Purpose
Features	Scroll, Zoom, Envelope, Bullets, and Macros Help buttons
Font	Font, Attributes, and WordPerfect characters buttons
Generate	Indexing, Table of Contents, and Table of Authorities buttons
Graphics	Graphics features buttons
Layout	Justification, Tab, Indent, Margins, and Styles buttons
Macros	Buttons to activate several useful WordPerfect macros
Merge	Buttons for creating and using merge files
Page	Page layout buttons
Tables	Buttons for creating and formatting tables
Tools	Buttons for activating items from the Tools menu
WP{WP}	Close, Open, Save, Print, Cut, Copy, Paste, Search, Font, and Speller buttons

Use the Quickmenu feature (see next tip) to choose one of these Button Bars.

Switch Button Bars using QuickMenu

 WordPerfect provides the Button Bar Quick-Menu so that you can change Button Bars more quickly.

To activate the Button Bar QuickMenu, position the mouse pointer anywhere on the currently displayed Button Bar and press the secondary (right) mouse button. WordPerfect displays a QuickMenu (see figure 5.1) that contains a list of all the currently defined Button Bars,

with a maximum of 20. Click the name of the Button Bar
you want, and WordPerfect quickly changes Button Bars
for you.

Fig. 5.1 *The Button Bar QuickMenu.*

You can also use the Button Bar QuickMenu to Hide (turn
off) the Button Bar, create a New Button Bar, Edit the
current Button Bar, or to select the Button Bar display
Options.

Display more buttons

By default, WordPerfect displays Button Bars across the
top of the document. However, you also can arrange the
buttons at the bottom, left, or right sides of the screen. In
addition, you can choose to display buttons with only the
pictures (icons) showing or with only the text showing.
Use QuickMenu to select Options, and select the setup
you want.

If you display buttons vertically at standard VGA resolution, you can show one additional button on your Button
Bar. If you also choose to display only Button Bar names,
you can display up to 21 buttons, which is 10 more than if
you show both text and pictures.

Rename the default Button Bar before modifying it

The default Button Bar is a file in the macros directory named WP{WP}.WWB. This bar is most useful as the initial, general purpose Button Bar. However, if you modify this (or any other predefined) Button Bar, then subsequently install an update to WordPerfect, you lose any changes you make because the WordPerfect's default Button Bar replaces your customized one.

To avoid this problem, and to maintain a copy of the original default Button Bar, immediately save the default Button Bar under a different name, and then make modifications only to the renamed Button Bar. Then you can safely add or remove buttons without fear of losing the Button Bar definition when you install a WordPerfect update.

Customize your Button Bar

To delete a button, or to add a new button to your *current* Button Bar, use QuickMenu to select Edit, or select View, Button Bar Setup, Edit. WordPerfect displays the Edit Button Bar dialog box (see figure 5.2). Note the name of the .WWB file you are about to change. If this file isn't the one you wanted to change, select Cancel and change Button Bars before proceeding.

Fig. 5.2 *The Edit Button Bar dialog box.*

- Remove an unneeded button by positioning the mouse pointer over it (the pointer changes to a hand holding a button), holding down the primary (left) mouse button, and dragging the button off the Button Bar.

- Add a new button by selecting the feature from menus. WordPerfect adds the button to the end of your Button Bar.

- To change the order of a button, drag it to its new location. WordPerfect adjusts the remaining buttons to accommodate the one you move.

Choose OK to save the changes, or Cancel to discard the changes.

Add macros buttons to your Button Bar

Using a button for a macro is much easier than selecting Macro, Play and then selecting the macro you want to use.

To assign a macro to the *current* Button Bar, follow these steps:

1. Use the QuickMenu to Edit the current Button Bar. If the Button Bar file shown in the Edit Button Bar dialog box is not the one you want, choose Cancel and change the Button Bar before proceeding.

2. Select Assign Macro to Button. The Assign Macro To Button dialog box appears.

3. Select the macro you want to assign to a button and then choose Assign. At the right end of your Button Bar, WordPerfect displays a button with the cassette tape icon and the name of your macro. You can change the position of the macro button by dragging the button to a new location on the Button Bar.

4. Choose OK to save the changes, or Cancel to discard the changes.

Change the macro button text

You can use a second macro to assign a macro to a button and also to change the text of the macro button. Suppose that you want to add a macro button that automatically adds a paragraph numbering code followed by an indent code. The macro is PARNUM.WCM, but you want the button to read ¶ Number. Follow these steps:

1. Record and save the macro you want to assign to the Button Bar. For example, save PARNUM.WCM.

2. Type and save the following macro (for example, save it under the name C:\WPWIN\MACROS\ADDBUTT.WCM):

   Application (WP;WPWP;Default;"WPWPUS.WCD")

   ButtonBarAddItem

   (

   ButtonText:"¶ Number";MacroName:"parnum.wcm"

)

   The ButtonBarAddItem contains two required parameters, one for the new button text, and another for the actual name of the macro being added to the Button Bar. Also, you can use WordPerfect characters (Ctrl+W) in the new button text.

3. Play the ButtonBarAddItem macro(ADDBUTT.WCM in this example), and WordPerfect adds the appropriate macro (PARNUM.WCM in this example) to your *current* Button Bar, displaying the enhanced text name.

6

CHAPTER

Formatting Documents

Although the content of your document should be your primary concern, with WordPerfect for Windows, you also can make plain-looking text attractive and easy to read. This chapter focuses on procedures that can help you produce documents that communicate more than just words.

Understand WordPerfect's default format settings and the codes that change them

WordPerfect, by default, assumes certain things about the format of your document. Understanding these default settings can make it easier for you to know how to modify the format of your text. Among the important initial settings are the following:

Top margin	1"
Bottom margin	1"

Left margin	1"
Right margin	1"
Tab stops	Every 1/2"
Line spacing	Single spaced
Page orientation	Portrait (8.5" by 11")
Font	Standard 10cpi Courier or equivalent (this setting may vary depending on your printer)
Page numbering	None

To change these settings, use formatting codes inserted in the document where the changes are to take place. Text that precedes the format code is not changed, and text that follows the format code is changed until WordPerfect finds another format code.

To change a whole document back to its original default setting, inserting a new code (for example, a margin setting code to 1") is not always necessary. Instead, delete the code that you changed from the default, and the document automatically returns to its default setting.

This process does not apply, of course, to situations where you leave the formatting code and later in the text need to change back to a default setting. Because you don't want to delete the earlier format change code, you need to add another format change code that resets the default setting.

Avoid accidentally deleting hidden codes

To prevent accidental deletion of important formatting codes, you can instruct WordPerfect to let you know about hidden codes and prompt you to delete them or not. Select File, Preferences, Environment, and select Confirm on Code Deletion.

Use measurements that match your ruler

WordPerfect displays all measurements in inches by default, but it uses decimal numbers for fractions of inches. Your own ruler probably can't tell you that 7/16" is the same as .437". Fortunately, WordPerfect enables you to enter several different types of measurement notations and then changes what you enter to decimal inches.

For example, suppose you want to enter a 1/2" margin. In the Margins dialog box, you can type any of the following:

.5" (decimal inches; the " is optional)

1/2" (fractional inches; the " is optional)

36p (points, 72 per inch; the *p* is required)

1.27c (centimeters, 2.54 per inch; the *c* is required)

600w (WordPerfect Units, 1200 per inch; the *w* is required)

WordPerfect automatically calculates the decimal equivalent of the unit of measurement you type and then displays that equivalent in the text box or in the format change code.

You can also use whole numbers and larger. For example, 1 1/2 is converted to 1.5". This conversion can be particularly useful when dividing a page into labels. For example, seven labels on an 11" sheet of paper is entered as 11/7; WordPerfect converts that number to 1.57".

Use Undo to correct a format change

If you mistakenly insert a format change code into a WordPerfect document, you can correct the mistake in two ways. One way is to delete the code. The only problem with this method is that automatically placed format change codes may be difficult to find quickly.

The second way is to choose Edit and then Undo
(Alt+Backspace). WordPerfect quickly and effectively
reverses the action you mistakenly took. Be careful,
however. If you don't undo the mistake immediately,
WordPerfect forgets what you did and can't correct the
mistake for you.

Find those pesky codes with Search

Use the Search feature to quickly find formatting codes.
Position the insertion point somewhere before the code
you want to find and follow these steps:

1. Turn on Reveal Codes by choosing View, Reveal
   Codes (Alt+F3). This step isn't necessary for the
   search, but it helps you see the code after you have
   found it.

2. Choose Edit, Search (F2 or use the Button Bar).
   WordPerfect displays the Search dialog box.

3. Choose Codes to display a list of WordPerfect codes.

4. If you know the name of the code for which you are
   searching, start typing that name. For example, type l
   and the cursor bar moves to L/R Margin.

5. When you locate the proper code, highlight it and
   choose Insert. WordPerfect places the format code in
   the Search For text box.

6. Select Search or press Enter to search for the code.

The search stops at the first code that matches. If the code
isn't found at all, a brief message appears on the status bar
saying String Not Found. If, after finding the code, you
determine in Reveal Codes that this code isn't the one for
which you are looking, continue the search by selecting
Edit, Search, Next (Shift+F2).

Use Document Initial Codes to format an entire document

When you insert a format change code into a WordPerfect document, the document changes from the point of the format code forward. The problem with this change is that other parts of your document, such as footnotes, don't receive the benefit of such code changes—even if the codes are at the very beginning of your document. To make such format changes global, you must make changes to Document Initial Codes, an unseen, but important part of every WordPerfect document. To access these codes, follow these steps:

1. Choose Layout, Document, and then Initial Codes. WordPerfect displays the Document Initial Codes editing window, which is identical in appearance to the Default Initial Codes editing window mentioned earlier. Any changes to WordPerfect's default codes made before this document was originally created appear in the lower part of the editing window.

2. Add the format code changes you want to the editing window in the same way you make such changes in a document.

3. Continue to add or delete codes until you are satisfied with your new document setting.

4. Choose Close (Ctrl+F4).

Note that you have changed the codes for only the current document but those changes now affect the entire document including headers and footers, footnotes and endnotes, and the body of the text.

To make changes to the default format code settings for all new documents, follow these same procedures after selecting File, Preferences, Initial Codes.

Quickly change old documents to new default format settings

If you are sure you want to change the default settings of an old document to your new settings, follow these simple steps:

1. At a blank screen, press the space bar. This action establishes a new document with your default Document Initial Codes.

2. Choose File, Retrieve. Then, select the file you want to change. Answer Yes to insert the file into the current document.

3. Backspace to remove the space you typed in step 1.

4. Save the document (choose File, Save, use the Button Bar, or press Shift+F3). You may want to give it a new name, just in case you need the original file.

Your document now has incorporated your current default settings and removed any initial default settings formerly attached to the older document.

Use Auto Code Placement

Certain format change codes belong at the beginning of a page and others belong at least at the beginning of a paragraph. WordPerfect is smart enough to know when a format change code can go anywhere in the document and when one should be automatically placed in the proper location.

Suppose you are typing a line and decide to change to double spacing. Without moving to the beginning of the paragraph, select Layout, Line, and Spacing. Type 2 in the Spacing text box (or choose 2.0 from the spacing icon on the Ruler bar). WordPerfect automatically inserts the [Ln Spacing: 2.0] code at the beginning of the paragraph you are typing, without moving your insertion point. You then can continue typing.

Several codes that are placed automatically at the beginning of a paragraph are Columns, Justification, Line Numbering, Line Height, Line Spacing, Left/Right Margins, Paragraph Numbering, and Tab Settings. Several codes that are placed automatically at the beginning of a page are: Top/Bottom Margins, Center Page, Page Numbering, and Paper Size. If a corresponding format code change already is located where the new code is to go, WordPerfect replaces the old code with the new one.

If you need to fine-tune your format change code placement by placing a code at a location other than the beginning of a paragraph or page, you must disable Auto Code Placement. Choose File, Preferences, and Environment; then deselect the Auto Code Placement check box in the Environment Settings dialog box.

Display the Ruler bar in all documents

Even if you turn on the Ruler bar display in one document, the Ruler bar does not automatically appear when you open another document. To make the Ruler bar always display as the default, choose File, Preferences, Environment; then choose Automatic Rulers Display.

Access features quickly by double-clicking the Ruler bar

 The complete dialog box for many formatting features can be accessed by double-clicking the feature's corresponding marker, button, or icon on the Ruler bar. The following table shows the results of double-clicking:

Ruler icon	Feature dialog box
Left or Right Margin marker	Margins
Table column marker (only when insertion point is within a table)	Table Options
Tab stop marker icons	Tab Set
Dot leaders button	Tab Set
Tab type icons	Tab Set
Font button	Font
Size button	Font
Styles button	Styles
Zoom percent button	Zoom
Table button	Table Create
Columns button	Define Columns
Line spacing button	Line Spacing

Abort a Ruler bar-selected setting by dragging the mouse above the Ruler bar

You may begin to use the Ruler bar to make a formatting change, but after clicking the button or icon, you decide against it. If you just release the mouse button, you may insert a format change code that you don't want. To cleanly abort a Ruler bar-selected format change, drag the mouse pointer upward, at least into the main menu area, and release the mouse button. The change does not take place.

Don't use spaces to align text

The brute force method of text formatting involves using spaces to push text around until it looks "pretty good."

Don't be fooled. Using tabs is the only way to assure correctly aligned text, even after you make font and format changes.

A tab moves the insertion point (and text) to the next available tab stop. Unusual changes in fonts (especially in font size) may affect how tabbed data lines up, but generally a tab to the 1.5" mark ends up at the 1.5" mark regardless of the type of font being used. When you use spaces, however, the printed version of your document may look very different from the on-screen version.

Learn to use Left Margin and Left Edge tabs

By default, WordPerfect's tab stops are set every 1/2" from the left margin. These tabs are called Left Margin (relative) tabs because as the margin moves so do the tab stops, always remaining in increments of 1/2" from the left margin. Thus, these tabs are relative to *all* margins, including the left margins of newspaper columns and table cells.

To make your tab stops always fixed relative to the edge of the paper (absolute) regardless of the margin settings, choose Layout, Line, and Tab Settings and click the Left Edge radio button in the Tab Set dialog box.

Change tab types using the Ruler bar

You can easily customize your tab stops by using the tab stop icons on the Ruler bar. For example, if you want a center-aligned tab at the 5" mark, position the mouse pointer over the center tab icon, which looks like a filled-in triangle, and drag to the 5" marker on the Ruler. Release the mouse button and the new tab stop replaces the normal left tab.

For your tab stops to have dot leaders, click the dot leader icon (it looks like an ellipsis) before changing the tab stop.

Remember to click the dot leader icon again to resume using regular tab stops.

Change tab stops for tabular data

Tabular data is characterized by columns of data separated by tabs. Consider the following:

Widgets	Bin A	3.45
Gadgets	Bin B	2.34
Thingamabobs	Bin C	15.47

You may be tempted to align the bin information by inserting two tabs between Widgets and Bin A and then only one tab between Thingamabobs and Bin C. Further, you may even consider adding an extra space before 3.45 and 2.34 to align them properly with 15.47. The only problem with this method is that changes in fonts, especially proportionally spaced fonts, may cause these columns to fall out of alignment.

Instead, all you need is a single tab between each of the columns and a special tab stop setting to align the number column properly.

You already know how to use the dialog box to change tab settings. You can change tabs more quickly with the Ruler bar, however. Follow these steps:

1. Position the insertion point anywhere on the first line of data (remember that Auto Code Placement places the tab setting code at the beginning of the line).

2. Move the mouse pointer to the tab stop marker on the Ruler that you want to remove.

3. Hold down the primary (left) mouse button and drag the tab stop marker downward off the Ruler and release the mouse button.

4. Repeat step 3 until you remove all unneeded tab stops.

5. Change the tab stop for the decimal number by dragging the decimal align icon to the tab stop location for the decimal numbers (see fig. 6.1).

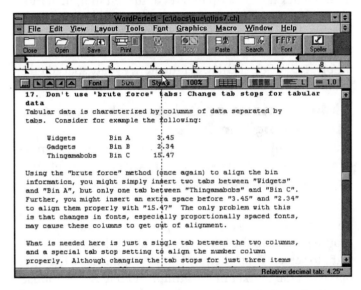

Fig. 6.1 *Changing a tab stop to a Decimal Aligned tab.*

6. Click and drag the tab stop markers to the left or right to align them exactly where you want them.

Set or reset evenly spaced tabs

If you change your tab settings to accommodate tabular columns of data, you probably need to change your tabs back to evenly spaced tabs for the rest of the body of your text. Even if you haven't changed your tab settings, you may want your tab stops to be closer together. For example, with proportionally spaced fonts, tabbed or

indented paragraphs look better with tabs of only 1/3"
rather than the default of 1/2".

To reset the tabs using the Ruler bar, first position the
insertion point where you want the tab setting to begin
(for example, after the columns of tabular data). Then
double-click the tab stop marker at the left margin of the
Ruler, and in the Tab Set dialog box, choose Clear Tabs.
Click the Evenly Spaced check box, and in the resulting
Repeat Every text box, type the interval you want (for example, 1/3"). Select OK to set the new, evenly spaced tabs.

Change, move or delete a group of tab stops using the Ruler

Changing individual tab stop markers on the Ruler can be
a tedious task. Fortunately, you can select a group of tab
stop markers and move, delete, or change them all at
once.

To select more than one tab stop marker, position the
mouse pointer to the left of the leftmost tab marker you
want to select. Then click and drag the pointer to the right
of the last tab marker in the group, and release the mouse
button (see fig. 6.2).

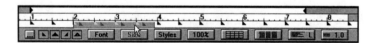

Fig. 6.2 *Selecting a group of tab stop markers.*

You now can do the following:

■ Change all the selected tab stop markers to a different type tab by clicking the appropriate tab type
icon.

■ Drag and move all the selected tab markers to a new
location.

- Drag the tab markers off the ruler, removing them altogether.

Note that if you move your mouse pointer anywhere except over the tab type icons or the selected group of tab stop markers, the pointer changes to the international No symbol. Clicking the mouse when this symbol appears cancels the tab marker selection.

Squeeze more lines onto a page by taking your lines to new heights

If you have ever created a letter or memo and ended up with just one line of extra text spilling over to the second page, you probably have wondered just how you can get the whole document onto the first page. You could change your margins or reduce the size of your font, but if you want to maintain your normal margins and font, turn to WordPerfect's Line Height feature.

You can reduce the line height ever so slightly without making it obvious to the reader that you have done so. But by reducing the line height, you also squeeze more lines of text onto the page. For example, to squeeze just two more lines of Courier text onto a page, follow these steps:

1. Position the insertion point at the beginning of the page (or top of the document).

2. Select Layout, Line, Line Height. WordPerfect displays the Line Height dialog box.

3. Select Fixed, and in the Fixed text box, replace .167 with .16 and select OK.

Check your page break and you'll see that two more lines of text are on the page, without seriously affecting the appearance of your text. Note that Line Spacing is always a multiple of the Line Height setting. Also remember that if you want the Line Height setting to affect your footnotes, place the Line Height format change code in Document Initial Codes (Layout, Document, Initial Codes).

Justify a whole block of text

If after creating a section of text, you decide you want to center it all, select the text and then turn on Center Justification.

Although you could choose Layout, Justification, and then Center to turn on Center Justification, you can save time and keystrokes by pressing Shift+F7 or Ctrl+J. To quickly apply Right Justification, press Alt+F7 or Ctrl+R. Also, Ctrl+L turns on Left Justification, and Ctrl+F applies Full Justification.

WordPerfect places a justification change code at the beginning of the block of selected text to apply the type of justification you requested. A second change code is placed at the end of the selected text to return it to its previous justification type. Any additional lines of text you add between these two codes are justified in the same way.

Make snazzy looking directory listings

You can create good-looking and properly aligned directory listings by using the Flush Right code. Select Layout, Line, and then Flush Right or press Alt+F7. Even better, add dot leaders by pressing Flush Right twice (Alt+F7) (see fig. 6.3).

Note that Reveal Codes does not indicate that dot leaders have been activated. However, if you want the dot leaders off, make sure the insertion point is anywhere to the right of the [Flsh Rgt] code and press Alt+F7 again.

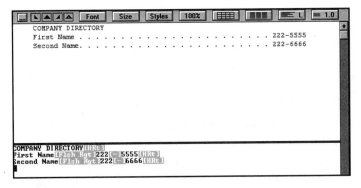

Fig. 6.3 *Directory listing using Flush Right with dot leaders.*

Using Flush Right is important because the phone numbers in figure 6.3 appear at the right margin and dot leaders fill the blank space in the middle regardless of margin or font changes.

Note that the Center code works the same way as the Flush Right code. If you position the insertion point anywhere on the centered text and press Center twice (Shift+F7), dot leaders precede the centered text. Using the same preceding steps, dot leaders also can be turned off.

Use Flush Right and Underlining to create fill-in-the-blank forms

If you have ever tried using the underline key to create fill-in-the-blank lines for forms, you understand the need to find a better procedure. The lines never quite reach the right margin; if they do, they wrap unexpectedly to the next line. Consider the following text:

NAME:_____

STREET ADDRESS: _____

To create perfect lines from the end of the text to the right margin, you must first enable underlining of tabs, then create underlined Flush Right codes.

First, position the insertion point somewhere preceding the lines you want to create (or better yet, place the following code in Document Initial Codes), and then select **Layout, Typesetting**. As you can see in the Typesetting dialog box, WordPerfect by default underlines spaces but not tabs (or center or flush right). Click the Underline **Tabs** check box and choose OK to insert the code in your document. Now WordPerfect underlines Tabs, Center codes, and Flush Right codes.

Next, position the insertion point at the end of the line of text (for example, following NAME:). Then, turn on underlining (Ctrl+U) and press Flush Right (Alt+F7). WordPerfect places a perfect line that is flush with your right margin.

The lines you create this way always extend completely to the right margin, regardless of whether you change the margins or the text to the left of the line. Likewise, the line never wraps to the next line.

Use underlined Tabs in fill-in-the-blank forms

Sometimes you want only partial lines across the page. Consider the following:

Name:_____   Phone:_____   City:_____

Set your tabs for the end of each line and the beginning of the next text item. Then type the text, turn on underlining (Ctrl+U) and press Tab to get an underline to the next tab stop. Be sure you turn on Underline Tabs as described in the preceding tip.

CHAPTER

Using Paper Sizes and Labels

WordPerfect assumes by default that you want to create your document in portrait orientation on a standard 8.5-by-11-inch sheet of paper. WordPerfect enables you to define and use additional paper sizes and shapes and to divide paper sizes into smaller units called labels.

This chapter focuses on the procedures that relate to defining and using paper sizes and labels.

Note that each printer has its own paper size definitions

When you add a custom paper size definition to WordPerfect, you do so only for the specific printer driver selected at the time. If you change printer drivers, the newly created paper size definition is no longer available.

For example, if you open a document that was created using a custom paper size definition for the WordPerfect printer driver, the document probably will not display or print properly using the Windows printer driver. Unless you have the exact same paper size definition in your currently selected printer, you must select the printer driver that does have that paper size or re-create the paper size for your current printer.

Add paper sizes even if you are connected to a network

If you try to add a paper size and are connected to a network, you may get error messages, or the paper size may disappear after you create it. These obstacles usually mean that the network administrator has protected the printer files (.PRS and .WRS) from being changed by users. Although this protection prevents users from deleting these files, it also prevents you from adding paper sizes.

Two easy solutions exist, both of which should be performed with caution and the blessing of your network administrator. One is to copy the appropriate .PRS and .WRS files from the network drive to your local hard drive. You then can make all the changes you want. The other is to ask the network administrator to add the page size to the network printer driver, a relatively simple task.

Share your .PRS and .WRS files with others

If you create special forms for your WordPerfect printer driver and then create a document using one of those forms, you still can share the file with someone else for editing or even printing. The advantage is that the printer need not actually be connected to the other computer in order to create or edit a document that takes advantage of the features of that printer. For example, you could create a file at home for printing at the office. All you must do is make sure the same .PRS file is on both computers.

To prepare to share a .PRS file with another person (or computer), follow these steps:

1. To determine which file to give the recipient, select File, Select Printer to display the currently selected printer.

2. Choose Setup to display the Printer Setup dialog box. At the top of the dialog box, you find the Filename (for example, HPLASIII.PRS). Choose Cancel to return to your document.

3. Select File, Preferences, and Location of Files. In the Location of Files dialog box, note the location for your Printer files (for example, C:\WPC). Choose Cancel to return to your document.

4. Select File, Open (F4). In the Filename text box, type the entire location and name of the .PRS file (for example, C:\WPC\HPLASIII.PRS).

5. Choose Options; from the pop-up list, select Copy. Copy the file to your floppy disk or a network drive, depending on how you intend to convey your document to the other computer. To avoid overwriting someone else's .PRS file, consider renaming it (for example, GILGEN.PRS). Also, copy the document you want to share to the same location. If the document is open on-screen, you may choose to Save As (F3) to that location rather than copying.

At the other computer, follow these steps:

1. The receiver determines a location for his printer files and then copies the files from your floppy disk or network drive to his own location. If WordPerfect prompts him to replace the .PRS file, he probably has a file by that name already and should use a different name to save your .PRS file.

2. The receiver selects File, Select Printer, and then chooses Add. WordPerfect displays the Add Printer dialog box.

3. From this dialog box, the receiver chooses the Printer Files (*.prs) radio button and selects from the Available Printers list the file name you provided.

4. The receiver opens the file. WordPerfect thinks the same printer is being used to edit the file, and the receiver then can make changes as if the actual printer were connected to his computer.

5. When the receiver finishes, if he doesn't have the same printer as you, he must copy the file to a floppy disk or to the network and return it to you. Otherwise, he can print the file himself.

If the receiver does return the document, he doesn't need to return the .PRS file because you already have it. You simply open the file he returns and print it.

Remember, if you do select a different printer to edit a document, you may need to reselect the printer you normally use before working with other documents.

Use WordPerfect's LABELS macro to set up commercial label types

You just bought a new box of laser printer labels and now you want to use them. You can search the WordPerfect Reference for instructions on setting up label definitions, or you can simply use the LABELS macro that comes with WordPerfect. Follow these steps:

1. Select Macro, Play (Alt+F10). In the Play Macro dialog box, type **labels** and choose Play. WordPerfect must first compile the macro, which may take a few moments. WordPerfect displays a dialog box asking whether you plan to use **Page** (laser) labels or **Tractor** feed (dot-matrix) labels.

2. WordPerfect now displays a list of more than 40 commercially available labels, including standard mailing labels, videocassette labels, shipping labels, and even name-tag labels. Select the item that matches your box of labels by clicking the entry with the mouse. More than one label may be selected at a time, and you may use the scroll bar on the right side of the dialog box to move up and down the label list. After you have finished making selections, select Install.

3. For each label type installed, the macro displays a dialog box asking whether the label type is Continuous, whether it's in a special bin of your printer or sheet feeder, or whether it must be fed manually into the printer. Choose the appropriate radio button.

4. WordPerfect then sets up a new paper size definition for the label type(s) you selected and asks whether you want to insert the definition(s) in your Document Initial Codes. To use a new definition now, select Yes. If you don't need it quite yet, select No.

After you set up a label definition, you do not need to run the LABELS macro again. When you need to use that particular label definition, select Layout, Page (Alt+F9), and Paper Size. Then choose the definition you need from the list.

Use labels for half-page brochures

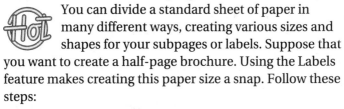
You can divide a standard sheet of paper in many different ways, creating various sizes and shapes for your subpages or labels. Suppose that you want to create a half-page brochure. Using the Labels feature makes creating this paper size a snap. Follow these steps:

1. Choose Layout, Page (Alt+F9), and then Paper Size.

2. Choose **Add**. WordPerfect displays the Add Paper Size dialog box (see fig. 7.1).

3. From the Paper Type pop-up menu, choose **Other**. In the Other text box, type the descriptive title of your new form.

4. Choose the Paper Orientation you want by clicking the icon that represents the landscape (sideways) orientation. WordPerfect automatically checks the Rotated Font check box and changes the Paper Size to `Stand Land, 11" by 8.5"`.

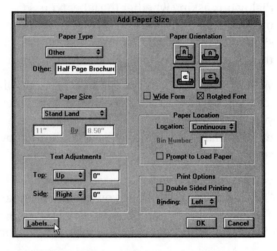

Fig. 7.1 *The Add Paper Size dialog box with the landscape orientation selected.*

You now have defined the larger page onto which you print your label pages. You need not make any other changes in the Add Paper Size dialog box unless you are using something other than continuous feed or you want double-sided printing.

5. From the Add Paper Size dialog box, choose **Labels**. WordPerfect displays the Edit Labels dialog box (see fig. 7.2).

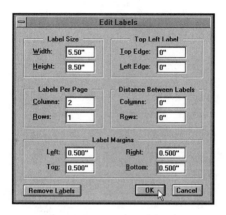

Fig. 7.2 *The Edit Labels dialog box set for two half-page labels.*

6. In the Label Size section, indicate the Width (5.5", or half the width of the landscape page) and the Height (8.5", or the entire height of the landscape page).

7. In the Labels Per Page section, indicate the number of Columns (2) and the number of Rows (1).

8. Make sure the Top Left Label and the Distance Between Labels sections are all set to 0".

9. Change the Label Margins to .5" on all four sides. This change may increase or decrease depending on your needs, but it can't be smaller than the amount allowed by the printer.

10. Choose OK, and then choose OK again in the Add Paper Size dialog box. The new form is now part of your printer definition file.

11. Choose Select to insert the new paper type into your document or Close to close the Paper Size dialog box.

When you use this definition, you get the page layout shown in the example in figure 7.3. Notice that each label page has its own headers and page numbers.

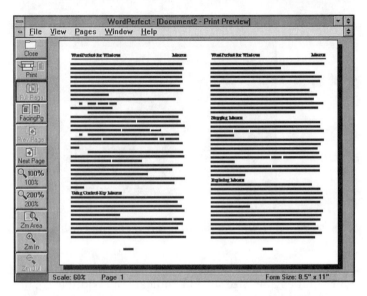

Fig. 7.3 *A sample half-page brochure using two labels on a landscape page.*

Place the Label Paper Size code in the Document Initial Codes

Suppose you want to print a mailing list of several hundred addresses onto sheets of labels. You have a secondary merge file (or other database) with all the information, and now you need a primary merge file for the labels themselves. After adding all the field codes and other punctuation, you need to add the Label Paper Size code. If you add it at the top of the primary merge file, however, the code will be replicated on each label of your merge. Instead, place the code in the Document Initial Codes of the primary merge file so that after the merge the code occurs only once in your document.

If you aren't creating a merged list but instead already have the list of addresses, make sure each address is separated by a hard page break. Then, all you need to do is add a Labels Paper Size code to the document. You might place this code at the top of the document, but to avoid accidentally moving the code to another page, place it in Document Initial Codes.

Center addresses on your labels

Remember that each label is a page as far as WordPerfect is concerned. As a result, you can use the Center Page feature to center your addresses vertically between the margins of your labels. Compare the two labels in figure 7.4.

Fig. 7.4 *Of the two labels, the address on the right label is centered.*

Unfortunately, placing the Center Page code in Document Initial Codes does not work except on the first label. Consequently, you must place this code at the top of each label page. For primary merge files, place the Center Page code at the top of the primary form. WordPerfect then replicates the code at the top of each individual label page, and each of your labels is nicely centered.

Use Advance codes for special forms

Some of the page sizes you create may be for use with specialized preprinted forms. When you use merge (from the keyboard or a secondary data file) to fill in such forms, you want your data placed at exactly the right position. You could use hard returns and tabs to try to align your text with the form, but an easier, more accurate way is to use the Advance feature.

First, use a ruler to measure the distance between the top and left edges of your printed form and the exact locations where you want your data (specifically, to the bottom, or baseline, and left side of your characters). Then choose Layout and Advance. Specify To Line for the vertical position and To Position for the horizontal position and insert the appropriate Merge Field or Input (keyboard) codes (see fig. 7.5). When you perform the merge, the data appears exactly where you want it.

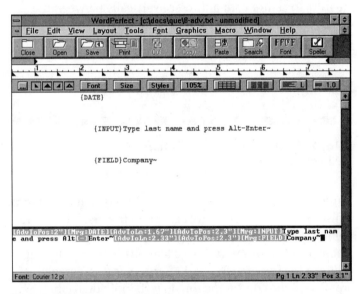

Fig. 7.5 *A document using Advance codes.*

Test print labels on regular paper

Labels are expensive. Get in the habit of doing a test run of your first page of labels on regular paper before using your sheets of labels. Remember that to print a page of 30 labels, you must print pages 1-30.

After printing your test page of labels, check for the following:

- Make sure the font size and style are what you expected and are appropriate for your labels.

- Check your labels' alignment by placing your printed page behind a page of labels and holding the pages up to a light. You then can tell whether the labels will print where they should.

- Make sure the page of information (for example, a mailing address) fits on the label without spilling onto the next label.

Create tickets using labels and page numbers

Creating tickets is easy using WordPerfect's labels feature. As shown in the tip on half-page brochures, just divide the full size page into smaller, ticket-sized pages (for example, eight columns and two rows on a landscape page).

Because each ticket is really a page by itself, you can use page numbers for your ticket numbers. You can repeat the ticket number on the ticket by inserting additional page numbering codes.

8

CHAPTER

Using Columns and Styles

This chapter on columns and styles completes the tips relating to formatting. Columns dress up your reports and newsletters; because columns shorten each line of text, they also make your material easier to read. Styles enable you to make your formatting consistent. You can include nearly any formatting procedure as part of a style, and then apply the style throughout a document or even in different documents.

Create newsletter text before adding columns

Because columns are easy to create and editing is much slower when columns are turned on, wait until you finish creating and editing your text before you add your news-paper-style columns.

Make columns of text even in length

Columns are easy to create, but how to manipulate them once they are turned on is not always obvious. One common problem that occurs on the last page of two-column documents is having one full column of text in the first column, but only a few lines of text in the second.

To make two columns of even length, first determine how many lines of text there are altogether and divide by two. For example, 54 lines in the first column plus 16 lines in the second column is 70 lines, and half of that total is 35.

Next, position the insertion point at the left of line 36 in the first column. Press Hard Page (Ctrl+Enter); you now have 35 lines of text in the first column and 35 in the second.

In columns, the Hard Page code acts as a column break instead of a page break, thus moving the remaining text to the beginning of the next column.

Adjust your column widths

By default, WordPerfect creates evenly spaced columns. You can adjust columns to nearly any width you please; the easiest way is to drag the column gutter marker to the right or left until you have the column widths you want (see fig. 8.1). You also can decrease or increase the size of your column gutters by adjusting (dragging) the column margin markers.

Use hyphenation with columnar text

Without hyphenation, lines can become terribly ragged when using columns. Before adding hyphenation, save your document. Then go to the top of your document and choose Layout, Document, Initial Codes. Then choose Layout, Line, Hyphenation, and choose Hyphenation On. Finally, choose Close.

Caution: After you hyphenate a document, the hyphenation codes remain even if hyphenation is turned off.

Don't save the file until you are sure you are happy with the hyphenation. If you aren't, close the file without saving.

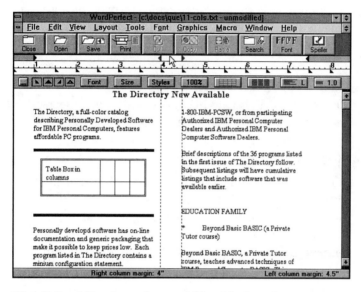

Fig. 8.1 *Adjusting column width with the column gutter marker.*

Use tables instead of parallel columns

You could take a long time learning how to define and use parallel columns, or you could simply create a table and enter the same data in the same format.

If you don't want the lines you get with tables, leave the lines until you finish entering the data (they help you see where you are working). After you finish editing, you can turn off all the lines. Position the mouse pointer against the left side of any cell (the pointer becomes an arrow) and click three times. The entire table is selected.

Then select Layout, Tables, Lines, and select None for both Inside and Outline lines.

If for some reason you really need parallel columns, save the document in the WordPerfect 5.0 format. Because that version did not support tables, WordPerfect converts tables into parallel columns.

Use styles to format text

Most people avoid styles because using them appears to be too difficult. Although styles do add a level of complexity to working with your documents, the benefits far outweigh the difficulties in most situations.

Consider, for example, the Bibliography style that comes with WordPerfect. Click the Styles button on the Ruler (or press Alt+F8) and select the Bibliography style. (If no styles are available, double-click the Styles button, choose Retrieve, and select LIBRARY.STY. Then repeat the above steps.)

WordPerfect formats the text of your bibliography entry in a hanging paragraph. When you press Enter, WordPerfect automatically advances two lines and is ready for the next entry.

Although this style is relatively simple, it illustrates the following important style-related points:

- **Consistency of format.** Whether you want the format to be the same from one document to another (for example, a series of newsletters) or throughout the same document (for example, section headings), styles can help. Describe the format once in a style; then, each time you use the style, the format is identical.

- **Ease of use.** Like a macro, using a style enables you to apply complex formatting information with just a few keystrokes. Depending on how heavily formatted your document is, using styles can save significant time.

■ **Ease of editing.** When you use a style, you can easily change any part of the style definition, such as font size, and all occurrences of that style update automatically. When you use a macro to set formatting codes, separate codes are placed at each location where the formatting is applied. Updating requires replacing each code with the new one separately.

■ **Reversion to document formats.** Style font changes always revert to the current document font, enabling you to change the Document Initial Font and have the changes affect the entire document. The same applies to other codes used in pairs.

Take time to learn how to use and create simple styles. After you begin to see the benefits, you may find you actually enjoy using them.

Create styles from existing codes

WordPerfect even helps you create a style *after* you insert the format codes directly into your document. Suppose you have a section heading that begins with a [Bold On] code followed by an automatic paragraph number and an indent code; the heading then ends with a [Bold Off] code. To place these codes in a style, follow these steps:

1. Turn on Reveal Codes (Alt+F3) to more precisely select the codes you intend to include in the style.

2. Select all the codes and text that make up the section heading.

3. Double-click the Styles button on the Ruler bar or select **L**ayout and **S**tyles (Alt+F8) to bring up the Styles dialog box.

4. Select Create to bring up the Style Properties dialog box.

5. Type a brief Name (for example, **Section**) and a longer Description (up to 54 characters). Also choose Style Off from the Enter Key Inserts pop-up menu if you want the Enter key to turn off your style.

6. Choose OK. WordPerfect places only your formatting codes (no text) before the comment box in the Style Editing screen (see fig. 8.2). If you want your style to end with the insertion point on the next line, place a Hard Return code after the comment box.

7. Close the editing screen and select Close again to return to your document.

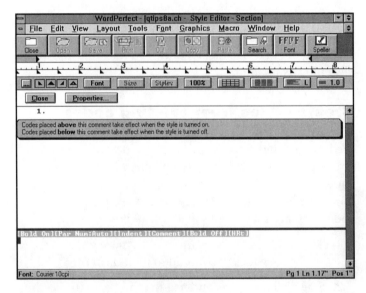

Fig. 8.2 *Editing a style.*

To use the style for a new section heading, click the Styles button on the Ruler and select Section from the list. Type the text of your section heading and press Enter.

Save your styles

WordPerfect stores the styles you create in style libraries, which are files you specify (for example, LIBRARY.STY). When you create a new style, WordPerfect adds it to your current document's list of styles but does not update any style files. Instead, you have to update manually by selecting Save As while in the Styles dialog box. The Save Styles dialog box appears. Select the file you want to update or type a new file name in the Save As text box (for example, NEWSLTR.STY). Choose Save; then choose Close to return to your document.

Keep your related styles in different library files

Although you can store all of your styles in one library file, consider saving the styles for each activity in separate library files if you have more than one unrelated activity. If you use one of the style libraries more frequently, you can specify that library as the default style library. Select File, Preferences, Location of files, and in the Styles Filename text box type the entire path and name of your library (for example, C:\WPWIN\NEWSLTR.STY).

To use a different style, press Alt+F8 or double-click the Styles button on the Ruler bar. Select Retrieve, and then select the name of the library you want to use. You may receive an error message indicating that a style by the same name exists and asking whether you want to replace it. If you know the new style is the same as the current one or if you know you haven't used the current one, choose Yes.

Start with a styleless document

Starting each document with a default library style has certain disadvantages:

- Retrieving other style libraries may cause conflicts with existing styles.

- Removing styles from the current document to unclutter the style list is a tedious process because you have to delete each style individually.

Instead, change your preferences so that no style comes up when you begin a new document. Select File, Preferences, Location of files, and in the Styles Filename text box, delete any name that may already be there. Choose OK.

When you begin a document, WordPerfect now displays No Styles Available when you click the Styles button on the Ruler bar. To select a Style Library file, double-click the Styles button (or press Alt+F8) and then select Retrieve. Select a Style Library File and choose Close. Those styles now appear in the pop-up list when you click the Styles button.

9

Applying Fonts and Attributes

This chapter focuses on factors such as typefaces, attributes, size, and even a few typesetting procedures, which determine the way your text appears.

Select the font that communicates best for you

In most cases, you should choose one basic font for your document. You can use variations, such as italics, small caps, and so on, but a single, consistent font throughout a document appeals to a reader much more than a hodge-podge of randomly selected fonts.

Let your document's purpose dictate the font you choose. For narrative writing, a simple Times Roman may be your best choice. The plain Helvetica might work better in a directory or instruction manual. Save unusual fonts, such as Broadway or Cooper, for headlines, posters, and other documents that mainly attempt to get the reader's attention. Usually you settle on one or two basic fonts that work best for the type of documents you create most often.

Know what fonts you have

Chances are that you aren't really sure which fonts you do have. WordPerfect 5.2, for example, comes with the Adobe Type Manager and several display fonts, such as Broadway and Hobo. In Windows 3.1, you have a set of TrueType fonts that you can size as you need and to which you can add several attributes, such as bold and italic. Your printer probably has a few internal fonts as well.

Your WordPerfect 5.1 and 5.2 printer drivers reflect the internal fonts, font cartridges, and any downloadable fonts you installed. The Windows printer drivers reflect the fonts that have been set up for all of your Windows programs.

To see just which fonts you have, first select the printer driver you want to use. Select File, Select Printer, and then choose either the WordPerfect or the Windows Printer Drivers. Then, select Font, Font or press F9.

If your printer fonts have corresponding screen fonts, you can see the fonts you select in the WYSBYGI ("What You See Before You Get It") window at the bottom of the list box. Most Windows fonts have matching screen fonts, but many WordPerfect printer fonts do not. To exit the Font dialog box without selecting a font, select Cancel.

Use Document Initial Font to change fonts

 WordPerfect documents all contain a document "prefix," a hidden part of the document with initial document formatting codes, information about the printer selected, and the initial font in effect when the document is created.

If, for example, you change the main font of your document from Courier to Times Roman by inserting a font code at the beginning of your text rather than using Document Initial Font, you can end up with Courier page numbers and footnotes and Times Roman text.

To determine the Document Initial Font for your current document, select Layout, Document, Initial Font. WordPerfect displays the Document Initial Font dialog box, identical to the font portion of the Font dialog box. The currently selected font is highlighted. Highlight the font you want and choose OK.

Now your text body matches your page numbers, as well as your headers, footers, and footnotes.

Create an Init Font button on your Button Bar

Instead of selecting Layout, Document, Initial Font to get to the Document Initial Font dialog box, you can save time by adding an Init Font button to your Button Bar to accomplish this task. Refer to Chapter 5 for information regarding this procedure.

Change your printer's default font

When you first install WordPerfect, the default font most often is a standard, fixed pitch font such as Courier. Generally, this font is a good choice for basic text typing and editing; you add font changes and other formatting choices later.

If you want a different default font for all new documents, however, change the Initial (default) Font for your printer driver. If you are changing a WordPerfect printer driver, follow these steps:

1. Select File, Select Printer. WordPerfect displays the Select Printer dialog box.

2. Make sure that the printer you want to change is selected, and then choose Setup. WordPerfect now displays the Printer Setup dialog box.

3. Choose Initial Font. WordPerfect displays the Printer Initial Font dialog box.

4. Choose the font you want as your new default font, and choose OK.

5. From the Printer Setup dialog box, choose OK, and then from the Select Printer dialog box, choose Select to save the changes and return to your document.

The procedure for changing the Initial Font for a Windows printer driver is slightly different:

1. Select File, Select Printer. WordPerfect displays the Select Printer dialog box.

2. Make sure the printer you want to change is selected, and then choose Select.

3. Select File, Select Printer once again. This time the Initial Font button is active.

4. Select Initial Font. From the Printer Initial Font dialog box, choose the font you want as your new default and then choose OK.

5. From the Select Printer dialog box, choose Select to save the changes and return to your document.

Assign your most used fonts to the Ruler bar

Although Document Initial Font is the best choice for global font changes, at times you need to quickly change back and forth between one font and another. Instead of selecting a commonly used font from your long list of fonts, you can instead assign such fonts to the Font button on the Ruler bar.

Double-click the Font button on the Ruler bar. In the resulting Font dialog box, choose ASSIGN to Ruler. The Ruler Fonts Menu dialog box appears. Select a font you want to add to the menu and choose ADD. Repeat this process for all fonts you want on the menu and then choose OK to return to the Fonts dialog box. These fonts now appear on the Font button's pull-down menu (see fig. 9.1).

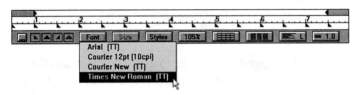

Fig. 9.1 *Selecting a font from the Font button on the Ruler bar.*

Caution: Don't add too many fonts to the Ruler bar or you defeat the purpose of having a shortcut to commonly used fonts.

Use size codes to change sizes of the same typeface

Sometimes you need to change the size of a font for a title or section heading. To change the size of your text font, but not the typeface, use the Size feature. Select the text you want to change, choose Font, Size (Ctrl+S), and select the size you want. WordPerfect for Windows places the appropriate size on/off codes around the selected text.

The actual size and typeface you get depend on your printer:

- If your printer driver does not have larger or smaller fonts that match the font of the selected text,

WordPerfect substitutes the best it can both in terms of size and font type.

- If your printer driver uses scalable fonts, WordPerfect uses the following default percentages to determine the new size, relative to the font of the selected text:

Fine	60%
Small	80%
Large	120%
Very Large	150%
Extra Large	200%

Perhaps the biggest advantage to using size instead of font codes is the time you save if you have to change the Document Initial Font. For example, if your document is in Helvetica, and then you change your Document Initial Font to Times Roman, text that was changed using size codes also changes to Times Roman. Text that was changed using font codes remains in the font to which it was changed.

Another reason for using size codes is that if you send your document to someone else, font codes may not convert at all. Size codes, however, adapt to whatever text font is chosen.

Caution: You can use the Size button on the Ruler bar you only with scalable fonts and only when you actually want to insert a specific sized font code. Don't use the Size button for the size changes discussed in the preceding paragraph.

Change size percentages to suit your taste

If the previously listed size percentages don't meet your needs, you can change any or all of them. Select File,

Preferences, Print. In the Print Settings dialog box, change
the values for the Size Attribute Ratios.

Note, however, that changes to Size Attribute Ratios affect
only documents created after the change is made.

Use attribute codes to change text appearance

For the same reasons listed in the tip on size codes, you
want to make attribute changes using attribute codes instead of changing the actual font. If you use, for example,
the italics attribute for a section of text, when you change
to a new initial or base font, that section changes to the
italic version of the new font.

Remember that commonly used appearance attributes
have keyboard shortcuts, such as **bold** (Ctrl+B), *italics*
(Ctrl+I), and underline (Ctrl+U).

Use size and appearance attributes to create "raised caps"

Books and magazine articles often use raised caps at the
beginning of a chapter or section. Raised caps are usually
a larger, bolder version of the typeface used in the rest of
the text (see fig. 9.2). To create a raised cap, follow these
steps:

1. Select the letter you want to change at the beginning
   of a paragraph using Select (F8), the mouse, or other
   selection techniques.

2. Press F9 and click or select the appearance and size
   attributes you want (for example, Bold and Extra
   Large).

3. Choose OK.

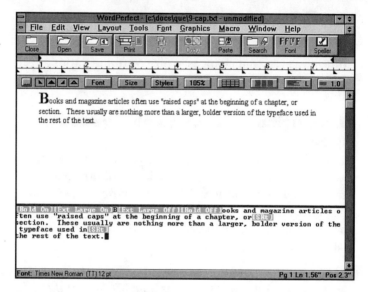

Fig. 9.2 *A raised cap using the bold and extra large attributes.*

Check the status bar

At the lower left of your screen on the status bar, WordPerfect displays the name of the current font with the same attributes in effect at the location of the insertion point.

Although you can use Reveal Codes to learn exactly where your insertion point is located, the status bar and the screen display can give you the same information.

For example, the status bar displays the font name in bold italics. Press the right arrow key. If the status bar now displays the name in italics only, you know that the insertion point is to the right of a Bold Off code, but still to the left of an Italic Off code. When you get used to the status bar, you will depend much less on Reveal Codes to accurately position your insertion point.

Use WordPerfect's special fonts to add pizazz

WordPerfect for Windows 5.2 comes with a dozen Adobe Type 1 fonts that can add pizazz to headlines, posters, and signs. You install these fonts separately from WordPerfect, and any Windows program can use them. However, the WordPerfect printer drivers cannot use these fonts, even in WordPerfect for Windows.

These fonts are scalable, which means that you can select the font and choose nearly any size, from less than a point to several hundred points. Figure 9.3 shows the typefaces you can choose for WordPerfect for Windows 5.2.

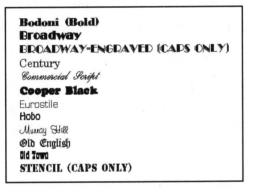

Fig. 9.3 *WordPerfect for Windows 5.2 Adobe Type 1 fonts.*

Use the Redline attribute to get shaded text

On some printers, mostly laser printers, redlined text prints out with a gray shaded background. The only way you can tell whether your printer does is to try it. Select the text to be redlined, and choose Font, Redline. On-screen, the text appears red, but when the text prints, it appears in gray.

Use WordPerfect's typesetting features for ultimate font control

One of WordPerfect's outstanding strengths is its typographic controls. Select Layout, Typesetting to see the Typesetting dialog box, which offers several document polishing features that you may not know about:

- Word Spacing determines the amount of white space inserted between words. If you don't think WordPerfect's guess is best, set your own percentage.

- Letterspacing determines the amount of white space inserted between letters. To squeeze just another character or two on a line, you can slightly decrease the percent of optimal from 100%.

- Word Spacing Justification Limits determines how much words can be compressed or spread apart when Full Justification is set.

- Line Height (Leading) Adjustment determines the amount of white space inserted between lines of text. A different setting is available for lines within a paragraph and for lines between paragraphs.

- Underline determines whether WordPerfect should underline tabs and Center and Flush Right codes.

- Kerning enables you to tighten up headlines to remove the appearance of extra white space between some characters.

- First baseline at Top Margin places the bottom of the first line at the top margin (instead of at the top of the first line).

- Printer Command sends any special commands your printer needs to exercise even greater control over your text.

Use kerning to "tighten" headline text

Note the extra white space between the W and the A in the first line of figure 9.4. After automatic kerning is turned on in the second line, the two characters are moved closer together.

ALL CALL FROM MWALL

ALL CALL FROM MWALL

Fig. 9.4 *Two headlines, the second of which is kerned.*

When automatic kerning is not quite enough, turn to manual kerning. First, position the insertion point between the two characters you want to adjust, for example, between W and A. Select Layout, Typesetting, Manual Kerning. WordPerfect displays the Manual Kerning dialog box, and displays the insertion point between the W and the A. As you decrease the Amount, WordPerfect graphically moves the two characters together (see fig. 9.5). When the adjustment is just right, choose OK. Choose OK again to save the changes.

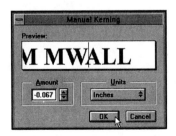

Fig. 9.5 *The Manual Kerning dialog box.*

10

Printing

In spite of promises of the "paperless office," for the foreseeable future printing will remain an important aspect of word processing. This chapter focuses on procedures that make printing easier and more effective.

Save a tree (part I): know your printer

A lack of understanding about the way the printing process works and, in particular, about the way the printer does its job results in printing errors and wasted paper. You can reduce this waste by learning all you can about your printer. Read your printer manual or talk with others who own or use similar printers. Understand what types of printing your printer can, or cannot, do.

Also, learn how to activate the printer's internal, cartridge, and downloadable fonts. If WordPerfect isn't properly set up for your printer, the printed page doesn't turn out the way you expect, even if the document appears correct on-screen. Finally, keep your printer in good repair. Paper jams and smeared printing from bad ribbons or toner cartridges result in wasted paper and wasted time.

Save a tree (part II): use Print Preview

Although WordPerfect for Windows shows you graphically how your document looks, you won't see some things until you print your document, even if your printer is set up properly. For example, the position and style of your page numbers do not appear on your editing screen.

Print Preview uses the printer definition file you selected to display the document almost exactly as it prints on paper. Before you print your document, choose File, Print Preview (Shift+F5) and review for the following:

- **Page layout.** In Full Page view, you determine whether margins, spacing, headers, footnotes, and page numbers are in their proper location. If Windows is set at standard VGA resolution, most text appears as solid thick lines. Higher resolutions, SuperVGA and better, may show text with actual characters.

- **Content layout.** In 100% view, you see actual text for the top half of the page, and you can check for line and page breaks. To see the lower half of the page, press PgDn (the scroll bar is much too slow). To see the next or previous page, press Alt+PgDn or Alt+PgUp, respectively.

- **Document layout.** To see how pages look when facing each other (for example, double-sided printing), use Facing Pages. You always see the even numbered page on the left and the odd numbered page on the right.

Zoom around in Print Preview

In Print Preview, you can zoom in on any part of your text that needs closer attention. 200%, Zoom In, or Zoom Out are three tools that enable you to do so, but Zoom Area is particularly useful for focusing on a specific part of the page. Select the Zoom Area button, position the cross-hairs at one corner of the area you want to see, and then drag the mouse to the other corner. Using this method, you can focus up to 400% of normal size.

You don't have to zoom back out to see other parts of your page. Simply click the preview screen and a small overview appears. Then drag the zoom box to the area you want to see and release the mouse button.

Place non-printing codes before printing characters at the top of your document

With Print Preview, you can easily catch the common mistake of accidentally placing a printable code before non-printing codes such as Paper Size, Headers, Page Numbers, and so on. Such a mistake means that the non-printing codes do not take effect until the *next* page.

To correct the problem, remove or reposition any printable codes so that the Paper Size code is first on the page. Better yet, place such codes in Document Initial Codes whenever possible.

Prepare your document for someone else's printer

You may have a trusty but unimpressive dot-matrix printer. You arrange with someone else to use a laser printer for the final copy. You can prepare your document ahead of time by installing and selecting the printer driver for that person's printer, even though it is not attached to your computer. Follow these basic steps:

1. If your target printer uses a WordPerfect printer driver, install that driver on your computer using the WordPerfect Install program.

If the target printer uses a Windows printer driver, install that driver on your computer from the Control Panel in Windows. If you set the Windows printer to LTP2, you can avoid accidentally printing to your local printer, which probably is connected to LPT1.

2. Select the target printer (File, Select) from your list of available (installed) printers.

3. Create the document using the fonts and other capabilities of the target printer. Use Print Preview frequently to see how the document will appear when printed on the target printer.

4. Save the document and reselect your own local printer to continue working with your own, locally printed documents.

The .PRS file (printer resource file) for WordPerfect printer drivers and the .WRS file (Windows resource file) for Windows printer drivers are what makes this procedure work. If these files are the same on your computer as on the computer connected to the target printer, your file will print just as you expect it to.

Share .PRS files

To print a document using someone else's printer (and their WordPerfect printer drivers), ask that person to give you a copy of his or her .PRS file (for example, HPLASIII.PRS for the HP Laserjet III), and copy that file to the directory that contains your own .PRS files. Check File, Preferences, Location of files to determine where this directory is. If you are connected to a network, check with your network administrator before copying printer files.

To install a printer using an existing .PRS file, select File, Select Printer, Add, and choose Printer Files (*.PRS). From the list, choose the appropriate .PRS file, and select Add.

You now can select this printer and format your document as if the printer were actually connected to your computer. Just use Print Preview frequently to see how the document will appear, even though you can't print it yourself.

Use WordPerfect for DOS's printer drivers

If you have been using WordPerfect for DOS, you can use the same printer drivers with WordPerfect for Windows. This convenience is especially useful if you made substantial changes to the 5.1 PRS files, such as adding Paper Size definitions.

Check the location of your WordPerfect for Windows printer files (File, Preferences, Location of files) and copy or move your WordPerfect for DOS .PRS files to that location. If you do this and plan to continue using WordPerfect for DOS, change the location of your printer files in WordPerfect for DOS (Shift+F1, Location of Files) to the WordPerfect for Windows location.

Caution: If you are connected to a network, check with your network administrator before changing printer file locations or copying .PRS files.

The main drawback of using WordPerfect for DOS's printer drivers is that you can't use the Adobe Type Fonts that come with WordPerfect for Windows 5.2. Consider the ultimate needs of your document before you choose your printer driver.

Print faster with WordPerfect printer drivers

Although WordPerfect printer drivers (.PRS files) often don't take full advantage of special fonts that Windows has to offer, they usually print much faster than the Windows drivers do.

If your font needs can be handled by WordPerfect for DOS printer drivers, and if your document contains many graphics, font changes, or tables, use the WordPerfect drivers. With documents of this sort, printing can be dramatically faster.

Use Ctrl+P to print an entire document

If you are sure your document is ready to print and you want to print the entire document, press Ctrl+P. Be careful, though. If you printed the document already and changed a setting (such as number of copies), Ctrl+P uses the changed settings, which may not give you what you expect. In this case, press Print (F5) and check the settings before proceeding.

Print a draft copy

Although you are as environmentally conscientious as the next person, sometimes you can get a better sense of your document as a whole (especially a long document) with a printed copy than you can by proofreading on-screen.

Print selected pages of a document

Suppose that you print your draft and find that minor changes are needed only on page 6, pages 8-10, and page 15. If these changes do not affect subsequent pages (for example, by the addition or deletion of large amounts of material), you can print only the pages you need. Follow these steps:

1. Press Print (F5).

2. Select Multiple Pages, and then select Print. The Multiple Pages dialog box appears.

3. In the Range text box, type the page numbers you want to print (for example, 5,8-10,15) and select Print. Do *not* include spaces between the numbers in the Range text box, or only the first set will print.

Printing multiple pages is also useful when you print a page of laser-printed labels. Because WordPerfect considers each label a single page, you must select Multiple Pages and specify **1-30** in the Range text box to print a page of 30 labels.

Print just odd or even pages

Suppose that you want to print your document on both sides of the paper, but can't afford that fancy new duplexing printer. WordPerfect enables you to print all the odd pages, turn the pages over, and run them through the printer again as WordPerfect prints all the even pages. Follow these steps:

1. Press Print (F5).

2. Select Multiple Pages and then select Print. The Multiple Pages dialog box appears.

3. In the Range text box, type the page numbers you want to print (for example, 1-, which means to start with page one and continue to the end of the document).

4. From the Odd/Even Pages pop-up menu, select Odd, Even, Logical Odd, or Logical Even.

5. Select Print.

The "logical" odd or even pages refers to any page numbering changes you may have made to your document. The regular odd and even pages settings disregard your page numbering and count sequentially from the beginning of the document.

Specify multiple copies

By default, WordPerfect generates each printed copy of your document. For example, if you want to print three copies of a complex table, WordPerfect generates the first copy and prints it, then the second, and so on. With a dot-matrix printer, this procedure is your only option.

Most laser printers, however, can accept the data for a document and, like a photocopier, make additional copies from the same image. The same applies to network printers, because most networks and network printers can produce multiple copies. From the Print dialog box, specify that multiple copies are to be generated by the printer. This specification dramatically reduces the printing time for multiple copies.

One disadvantage to this method is that the multiple copies are not collated when you finish printing because the printer makes all copies of one page before it proceeds to the next page. But this price may be small, considering the time saved in printing.

Print final graphics in high resolution

By default, WordPerfect prints graphics in medium instead of high resolution, which saves significant time for dot-matrix printers when printing draft copies, but does not usually save laser printers much time. When printing final copies, however, set the resolution to high.

Remember that graphics settings can affect text quality

WordPerfect's character sets consist of some 1500 characters, most of which are not native to your printer or even to soft fonts or printer cartridges. Such characters, as well as text found in equations, are generated graphically, and the Graphics Quality setting, in addition to the Text

Quality setting, can determine whether they look crudely constructed, whether they look polished like the other text in your document, or whether they print at all (Do Not Print).

If the Text Quality is set to High, all graphically created characters print in the highest quality, even if Graphics Quality is set to Low or Medium. But if *neither* Text Quality nor Graphics quality is set to High, the quality of the graphically generated text can be noticeably inferior. WordPerfect and Windows print drivers also handle these special characters somewhat differently, as noted in the following table:

If graphics quality is:		The printed result is:	
Text	Graphics	WordPerfect	Windows
High	High	High	High
High	Medium	High	N/A
High	Low	High	N/A
Medium	High	High	N/A
Medium	Medium	Medium	N/A
Medium	Low	Medium	N/A
Low	High	High	N/A
Low	Medium	Medium	N/A
Low	Low	Low	Does not print

Change your default print settings

If you commonly use print settings that are different from the defaults, save yourself time by changing the default print settings. Select File, Preferences, Print to display the Print Settings dialog box. Make the appropriate changes and select OK. Note that changes made to print settings affect only the way that new documents print. Those documents created and saved before you made the changes use the old print quality settings when you open and print them.

Make sure your printer has enough memory to print graphics

If you have several graphics or a lot of graphically generated text on a single page of your document, only part of the page may print. This problem usually occurs because your printer (not your computer) does not have enough memory to set up an entire page before printing. For example, many laser printers come with only 512K memory, but it takes 2M or more of memory to print full-page graphics. If you run into this problem, either reduce the graphics you include on one page, or purchase additional memory for your printer.

Use Binding Offset for bound pages

To print pages on both sides of the paper and bind the pages in a notebook or other type of bound document, you can use Binding Offset to allow extra space at the edge of the printed page. Press Print (F5) and type the offset amount in the Binding Offset text box.

11

CHAPTER

Using Tables

The capability to create and format tables is one of the most versatile and useful features in WordPerfect. Although tables are extremely easy to use, many people are afraid to try them because they think that tables are just too complicated. If you have never created a WordPerfect table, find out what tables are all about. Even if you have used them for some time, you will find several useful tips in this chapter.

Use the Tables Button Bar

 New with WordPerfect 5.2 is a series of specialized Button Bars, one of which is specifically designed for working with tables (see fig. 11.1). Because the actual menu commands for tables are buried deep in WordPerfect's menu system, working with tables using menus can be painfully slow and difficult. The Button Bar puts table commands just a mouse click away, which makes working with tables quick and easy.

Note: This chapter assumes that you have selected the Tables Button Bar.

Fig. 11.1   *The Tables Button Bar.*

Use the Ruler to create tables

Creating a table is relatively simple using the Button Bar or even the menus: specify the number of rows and columns you want. Using the Ruler, however, is even easier.

Click and hold the Tables icon on the Ruler and then drag the mouse pointer until you form the grid of rows and columns you want. When you release the mouse, WordPerfect creates the table you defined. By default, WordPerfect displays a grid that suggests you are limited to 10 rows by 10 columns. You can drag the mouse farther, however, to create a table of up to 43 rows (on a Standard VGA screen, with the Button Bar selected) by 32 columns.

Although you are limited to 32 columns, you can have a virtually unlimited number of rows. If you need more than 43 rows, create your table using the Button Bar or the menus and specify the larger amount.

Use the Ruler to adjust the table size

When the insertion point is inside of a table, the margin indicators on the Ruler refer to the column dividers in the table. Double-click any of these margin indicators, and WordPerfect displays the Table Options dialog box that you can use to change the number of rows and columns in your table. Note that when you increase the table's size, rows are always added to the bottom of the table and columns to the right.

Turn regular tabular text into tables

One of the quickest and most impressive changes you can make to a report is to convert regular tabular data into a table.

To convert a list of tabular data into a WordPerfect table, select the entire list, using the mouse or keyboard, and then double-click the Table button, or choose Layout, Tables, Create. WordPerfect displays the Convert Table dialog box. Select Create Table from Tabular Column, and WordPerfect instantly produces a table.

If the table doesn't look quite right (it probably won't), just drag the column and margin markers on the Ruler to adjust the width of the table and columns (see fig. 11.2).

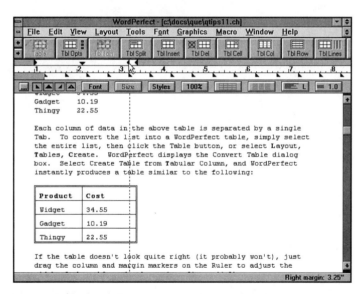

Fig. 11.2 *Using the column and margin markers to adjust the layout of a table.*

Caution: Make sure your tabular columns are separated by just one tab each. You may have to set your tab stops and remove some extra tabs to accomplish this. If you don't, the data does not convert properly to a table and you have to do extensive table editing.

Move quickly and easily from one cell to another

The easiest way to move from one cell to another in a table is to use the mouse. Click in the cell to which you want to move.

You also can move quickly forward, one cell at a time, by pressing Tab, or move backward by pressing Shift+Tab. To move up or down one row at a time, press Ctrl+↑ or Ctrl+↓.

Put a tab in a table cell

Normally, when you press Tab while in a table, the insertion point advances to the next cell to the right. If you want to insert a tab code in the actual table cell, press Ctrl+Tab.

Use a table cell rather than a text box

You can use a regular table cell in place of a text box (graphics box) to quickly set off a paragraph of text, a title, or anything else you want to highlight. You then can size the box by dragging the margin markers and change its lines by clicking the Tbl Lines button or by choosing Layout, Tables, Lines (see fig. 11.3).

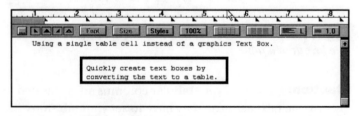

Fig. 11.3 *Using a single table cell instead of a text box.*

Use the mouse to select an entire cell, row, column, or table

To quickly select the contents of an entire cell, position the mouse pointer toward the left edge of the cell until a horizontal arrow appears (see fig. 11.4). Click once and the whole cell is selected.

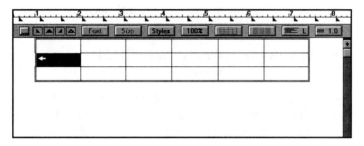

Fig. 11.4   *Using the mouse to select a cell.*

If you click twice, you select the whole row of cells. This procedure is useful when you want to format all the cells in a single row. (The Tbl Row button on the Button Bar will not format a single row.) It is also useful when you want to format all the columns in a table. After selecting the row of cells, click the Tbl Col button to format all the rows in each of the highlighted columns.

If you click three times, you select the entire table.

If you position the arrow at the top of the cell (where the arrow appears as a vertical arrow) and click twice, you highlight all the cells in a column.

Delete the contents or structure of a table

To delete a table from your document, you can select the table as you select any other text (begin selecting outside of the table and extend the selection beyond the other side of the table). Then press Backspace or Delete.

You also can click three times on the left edge of any of the table's cells to select the table. Press Backspace and in the Delete Table dialog box, select one of the following radio buttons and choose OK:

- Entire Table deletes the whole table, including content and structure.

- Contents deletes the text content, but leaves the structure of the table intact.

- Table Structure deletes the table's structure, but leaves the data. When you select this option, the [Row] codes convert to hard returns and the [Cell] codes convert to tabs.

Be careful, however. If you delete an entire table, or even if you leave the text, you cannot undo the action. Also, cell or column attributes of the table do not remain with your data.

Use Undo to restore columns or rows of deleted data

If you select a row, column, or group of cells and delete the contents of those cells, you cannot use Undelete to restore their text. Instead, immediately select Edit, Undo (Alt+Backspace).

Know the location of your table lines

Do you know where your table lines are? They probably aren't where you think. For example, Cell A1 (the cell in the upper left corner) has lines on only two sides—the left and the top. The lines that appear to be the bottom and the right are actually lines from adjoining cells (see fig. 11.5).

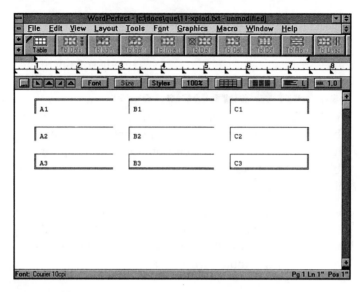

Fig. 11.5 *A disassembled table indicating table lines.*

For example, if you want a double line at the bottom of row one, you actually want to place a double line at the *top* of row two, replacing the single line that's already there. If you put the double line at the bottom of row one, you end up with a double line there and an *additional* single line under it at the top of row two. The single line gives the double line a shadow effect and can look nice, if a shadow effect is what you want.

Use header rows for long tables

If you create a long table, one that spans across a page break, you may want to use *header rows* (rows that repeat themselves at the top of every page, such as column labels).

Click the Tbl Opts button or double-click one of the table margin or column markers on the Ruler. After the Table Options dialog box appears, type in the Headers Row text box the number of rows you want as header rows. You count the number of header rows beginning at the top of the table.

Use Sort to sort table rows

WordPerfect knows when the insertion point is inside of a table. Thus, if you choose the Sort feature (Tools, Sort) while in a table, WordPerfect automatically sets up for a table sort. A table sort treats each row as a record and each column as a field.

Header rows are ignored during a table sort. Even if you have a short table, designating the top rows that you do not want sorted as header rows can be helpful when you plan to perform a table sort.

Lock table cells to prevent changes and speed data entry

To protect a cell from being changed, you can lock it by clicking the Tbl Cell button (or choosing Layout, Tables, Cell) and choosing Lock from the Cell Attributes area. Locking is particularly useful if you are using math formulas and don't want them to be modified or replaced by keyboard-entered data.

Locking cells also makes entering data into a table form easier. When you press the Tab key, the insertion point lands in the next unlocked cell, skipping over any locked cells. Only those cells that require data entry are left unlocked.

Use tables in newspaper-style columns

You cannot place a table directly into a newspaper-style column. Instead, you must first create a table box in the column, and create your table inside the table box.

Use graphics table boxes to place tables side by side

Try as you may, placing two tables side by side is impossible without placing them in graphics table boxes. Determine the amount of horizontal space that is available for each table, and then create a table box. Choose Box Position to set the Width (Automatic Height) and Horizontal Position (Margin, Left). Then create the table that goes in the table box. Repeat the process for the second table box, which you position at the right margin. Figure 11.6 shows the result of this procedure.

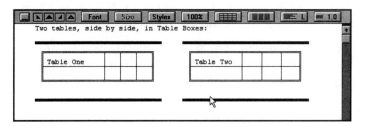

Fig. 11.6   *Two table boxes side by side.*

Make two tables look like one

Tables are great for creating forms; however, you may need one part of the form to have more columns than the other part. As long as you can join or split columns, you can create the entire form in one table. But if it begins to get too complicated, you might consider using two tables.

Two tables can be made to look like a single table by creating the second table immediately following the first. If you remove the bottom lines of the first table, the illusion is even greater.

The only drawback to using two separate tables is that numeric data from one table cannot be transferred or calculated in the other table. For printed forms, of course, this problem is of no concern.

Use fixed row heights for table calendars

Some forms require that rows and columns be exactly the same size, regardless of the data that goes into them. For example, a calendar form should not be allowed to expand beyond a page, but at the same time, you want blank rows (weeks) to be the same height as rows that have information in them. To solve this problem, use Row Height.

Position the insertion point in the row you want to set, or select all the rows in a column (for example, all the Sundays in a calendar form). Click the Tbl Row button or choose Layout, Tables, Row. WordPerfect displays the Format Row dialog box.

Choose the Multi Line, Fixed radio button and enter the height that you want for the calendar so that the rows neither grow nor shrink as text is added or deleted.

Use Drag and Drop to copy cell attributes

You can use Drag and Drop to copy cell attributes from one cell (or group of cells) to another. Click a selected cell and hold down the mouse button. Drag the mouse to the target cell and release the mouse button.

Caution: If the original cell has other than single lines at the right or bottom, those line attributes also are copied to the target cell.

Use your tables to create crossword puzzles

Tables are not only practical; they can also be fun. For example, you can use them to create games. Suppose you want to create a crossword puzzle like the one in figure 11.7. Create the number of rows and columns you want, and then follow these steps:

1. Set the column widths and fixed row heights to equal sizes (for example, .5").

2. Add shading to cells that will not be used for letters. (Click the Tbl Cell Button, and choose Shading.) Remember that you can add shading to one cell and then use Drag and Drop to copy the shading to other cells.

3. Click the Tbl Opts button and change the Shading percentage to 100% (solid black). Also, change the left and top cell margins (to .005", for example) so that text numbers can be placed closer to the corners. Then choose OK.

4. Choose a small font, or set the font attribute to Fine, and place numbers in each cell that begins a word.

Merge lists to a table

 Tables are ideal for lists. If you already have the data for your lists in a database (for example, a secondary merge file), you can merge to a table to create your lists. Suppose you want to create a three column table that lists in separate columns the name, city, and phone of each of your clients. Follow these steps:

1. Make sure the database is ready and determine the field names or numbers.

2. Create the basic table to which you intend to merge. In addition to any header rows, you should have three blank rows.

3. Use merge commands, similar to the ones seen in figure 11.8, that place the data from one record on the first blank row. The commands to loop back and add the data from the next record go on the second blank row. The last row remains blank. (See your WordPerfect reference for details on using merge commands.)

4. Save the primary file with your merge commands; then, from a blank screen, merge the file with your own secondary file or database.

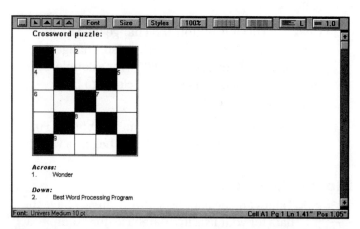

Fig. 11.7 *Using a table for a crossword puzzle.*

WordPerfect expands the table until the merge is complete. You end up with a couple of extra blank rows, which then can be deleted from the table. If you don't use an extra blank row in your primary form, the merged table will have double lines between each row.

CLIENT ROSTER		
Name	City	Telephone
{LABEL}Start~{ON ERROR}{GO}Quit~~{FIELD}Name~	{FIELD}City~	{FIELD}Phone~
{NEXT RECORD}{GO}Start~{LABEL}Quit~		

Fig. 11.8 *A primary merge table to create a merged table list.*

12

CHAPTER

Using the Speller, Thesaurus, and Grammatik

One of the first special WordPerfect features most people try is the Speller. However, many people never learn enough about the Speller (or the Thesaurus and Grammar checker) to use them effectively as tools for better writing. This chapter focuses on these three word-crafting tools.

Save the Speller for your final draft

You just banged out the first rough draft of your research paper. The temptation is to immediately run the Speller to catch misspelled words. Before you do, remember that you probably need to make many other revisions, including adding more text. If you spell check your document now, you only have to do it again later. To save time, run the Speller once just before you save for the last time and print.

Don't rely on the Speller to proofread your document

Remember that the Speller does not check for usage. If you write "I went to there party", the Speller reports that everything is spelled correctly. Although Grammatik, the grammar checker, may catch such errors, nothing substitutes for careful proofreading of your document.

Look up a word quickly with the Speller

WordPerfect's Speller can find words that are, look like, or even *sound* like the word you spell. To quickly look up a word, start up the Speller (select **Tools, Speller** or press Ctrl+F1). Don't select any buttons; instead, begin typing the word you think you want. For example, type **wurd**. You won't see any suggestions in the Suggestions box, but if you click the Suggestions button, WordPerfect tells you about "word", along with "warhead", "wart" and even "weird."

Use your supplementary dictionary for special terminology

If you have special words (for example, technical terms or proper names) that you use all the time, add them to your supplementary dictionary. Open a file that contains the special words, and run the Speller (select **Tools, Speller** or press Ctrl+F1). When the Speller stops at one of the unrecognized words, click Add. Continue until you check the entire list.

Your supplementary dictionary now contains the special names and terminology, and will never prompt you again to correct these words.

Remove incorrect words from the supplementary dictionary

 If you mistakenly add misspelled words to your supplementary dictionary, follow these steps to remove them:

1. Determine the location of your Supplementary dictionary by starting the Speller (Ctrl+F1) and choosing Dictionary, Supplementary. The name of the file you need is WP{WP}US.SUP. (If you are on a network, the name of the file is WP*xxx*}US.SUP, where *xxx* is your network identification.)

2. Then close the Speller and choose File, Open (F4). Type the full path and name of your supplementary file (for example, **C:\WPC\WP{WP}US.SUP**), and choose Open. Your supplementary dictionary lists words, one per line, in alphabetical order.

3. Delete the word you want to remove. Check for other incorrect words, or add words yourself (one per line, in alphabetical order).

4. Save the .SUP file (Shift+F3) and close the document (Ctrl+F4).

Create different types of supplementary dictionaries

Although your supplementary dictionary can hold many words, a large supplementary dictionary slows down the Speller. If you can separate the types of spelling you do, you can create additional supplementary dictionaries and select the one you want before you check your document.

Type a list of words, one per line, and save it in a document with a .SUP extension. Save this document in the same location as your regular supplemental dictionary.

To change to a different supplemental dictionary, run the Speller, and choose Select Dictionary, Supplementary. WordPerfect displays the Select a Supplementary Dictionary dialog box that includes a list of all .SUP files. Select the supplementary dictionary you want.

If you add words during the spell check, these are added to the new supplementary dictionary. Furthermore, the new supplementary dictionary remains in effect until you select another one, or until you exit WordPerfect.

Spell check just a portion of your document

Instead of spell checking an entire document, select just the text you want to check, and then start the Speller (select Tools, Speller or press Ctrl+F1).

Force the speller to ignore a section of your document

If your document contains a large section of unusual names or terms that the Speller won't find in its dictionary, and you don't want to add them to your supplementary dictionary, you can force the Speller to skip that section by placing a non-existent language code at the start of that section. Follow these steps:

1. Position the insertion point at the beginning of the section you want to skip.

2. Select Tools, Language. WordPerfect displays the Language dialog box. US is the United States English code, although if you are using another spelling module you may see a different Current Language code.

3. Select Other from the list, and in the Other text box, enter a non-existent language code, for example, ZZ.

4. Move to the end of the section you want to skip.

5. Repeat steps 2 and 3, but select the English-US code, or the code for the original language in use.

Now when you run the Speller, it displays an error message when it encounters the ZZ language code. Select Skip Language, and the speller continues but disregards the section marked with the ZZ language code.

Minimize the Speller, Thesaurus, and Grammatik

The Speller, Thesaurus, and Grammar checkers all are separate Windows programs, which you can use by themselves or with other Windows programs that recognize them.

To reduce the startup time for these programs, don't close them after you have opened them. Instead, minimize them by pressing Alt+Space, Minimize, or by clicking the Windows Minimize button. When you minimize, rather than close, these applications, they also remember any words you have skipped (in the Speller) or any headwords found (in the Thesaurus), which can save you additional time.

Caution: If you have relatively limited RAM (memory), this method can actually degrade Windows performance.

Use wild cards to look up words with the Speller

If you want to find words for which you know only part of the spelling, you can use wild cards in place of characters that you're not sure of. The * (asterisk) character is a wild card for a range (one or more) of characters, and the ? character is a wild card for single characters. For example, if you type t*ping and then click Suggest, you see words like taping, typing, and timekeeping. If you want to cheat on crossword puzzles, type the word, placing a question mark at the location of the missing characters, and click Suggest. For example, typing **ast?o?o??** returns astrodome, astrology, and astronomy.

Spice up your prose with the Thesaurus

Apparently most people are less preoccupied with being boring than they are with being correct. Perhaps that explains the popularity of the Speller, but the relative disregard most have for the Thesaurus. If you haven't tried using the Thesaurus to improve your word selection, do so. Just click a word that you use too frequently, and choose Tools, Thesaurus (Alt+F1). WordPerfect displays the Thesaurus, which displays a list of synonyms and antonyms.

Select the word you want, and choose Replace to paste it into your text.

Watch for Grammatik proofing files

If you use Grammatik regularly, you may notice extra files showing up on your hard disk with the .GBK file name extension. When you save your Grammatik edits, the program creates a backup of the pre-edited version. If you no longer need these backup files, you can delete them.

Use only one spell checker

If you already use the WordPerfect Speller, you can deselect the Grammatik spell checker by starting up Grammatik and then selecting Preferences, Options, and deselecting Suggest spelling replacements.

However, Grammatik's speller, Mor-Proof, does a few
things that WordPerfect's doesn't, such as offering suggestions based on grammar rather than just on word patterns
(for example "bought" would be suggested for "buyed").

Define a writing style for Grammatik

If you have written documentation for a computer
manual, you don't want Grammatik looking for the same
kind of prose you expect from a novel. From Grammatik,
select **Preferences, Style**. From the Writing Style dialog
box, select a writing style and a level of formality. You even
can customize a writing style to suit your own special
needs.

13

CHAPTER

Page Formatting, Referencing, and Sorting

A one-page memo is easy to follow, but long documents sometimes need navigational aids for the reader. A simple thing like page numbering, for example, can help a reader know how much she has to read, and, in the case of loose pages, make sure she reads everything in the proper order.

This chapter focuses on those tools that make it easier for the reader to navigate a document, such as page numbering, headers and footers, lists, cross-references, and footnotes. These tips apply to any document longer than a single page.

Use page numbers with style

By default, WordPerfect does not number pages, so you have to turn page numbering on and specify where WordPerfect should place the page number. Select Layout, **Page**, **Numbering**, and WordPerfect displays the Page Numbering dialog box.

Notice the Accompanying Text box with the [^B] code. WordPerfect places the current page number wherever it finds this code. You can add text before and after the [^B] to create a page number with a little style. Try Page [^B], -[^B]-, or IV-[^B] to get results such as Page 85, -85-, or IV-85.

You can't add attributes such as bold and italics with this method but it works fine for quick and simple changes in page numbering style.

Note: The accompanying text appears wherever you insert a page number, including indexes and tables of contents.

Place page numbers in footers (or headers)

If you don't want to use a page numbering style, or if you want to make your page numbering style more special, place a page numbering code in a footer or header. Create a footer (Layout, **Page**, **Footers**, **Create**) and in the Footer Editing Screen, click the Page Numbering button to insert the [^B] code. You can position this code anywhere you like and add any desired attribute or font changes. Choose Close when you are ready to insert the footer with the page number in your document.

Remember that the text of the footer or header takes on the same font as your Document Initial Font, unless you change it by inserting a Font code directly in the footer or header.

Include graphics in a header or footer

Headers and footers aren't just for text. Suppose that you want to include a simple graphic along with a graphic line and your company's address at the bottom of every page. Create a footer and then add each of these items to it just as you would add them to any document. Choose Close when you finish. The footer shown in figure 13.1, adds a graphic, a flush right address, and a graphic line.

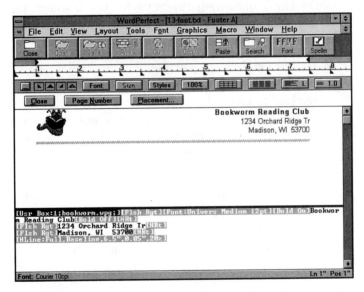

Fig. 13.1 *Creating a footer with a graphic character and a graphic line.*

Manually create short tables of contents

If your document has only two or three table of contents entries, you may save time by creating your table of contents manually, instead of using WordPerfect's Table of Contents feature. Type in your entries, press Alt+F7 twice to create flush right dot leaders, and type the page numbers for your entries. If you have several table of contents entries, however, use WordPerfect's Table of Contents feature.

Automatically generate tables of contents

WordPerfect enables you to mark sections of text to include in a table of contents, and then helps you automatically generate a table of contents, complete with page numbers. The steps are easy:

- **Define:** On the page you intend to use for the table of contents, select Tools, Define, Table of Contents. In the Define Table of Contents dialog box, select the number of levels you want (up to five, although one or two generally is sufficient), select the numbering style you want (the default is flush right numbers with dot leaders) and choose OK.

- **Mark:** Search throughout the document for the section headings you want to include in the table of contents (you can't include anything except already existing text). Select the text you want to include, select Tools, Mark, Table of Contents, indicate which level the entry should be (usually level one), and choose OK. Repeat these steps until you have marked every table of contents entry.

- **Generate:** With the table of contents defined, and the entries marked, you now generate the table of contents by selecting Tools, Generate. When asked whether you want to generate everything including the table of contents, answer Yes. WordPerfect finds and organizes your entries, including proper page numbers and the format you chose.

Create a style for table of contents entries

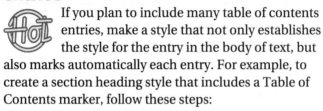 If you plan to include many table of contents entries, make a style that not only establishes the style for the entry in the body of text, but also marks automatically each entry. For example, to create a section heading style that includes a Table of Contents marker, follow these steps:

1. Double-click the Styles button on the Ruler bar, or select Layout, Styles, Create (Alt+F8). Give your style a short name and a longer descriptive name. Choose OK. WordPerfect now places you in the Styles Editing screen.

2. Enter the codes for your heading style. WordPerfect places those codes above the Comment box.

3. Press Select (F8) and move the insertion point to the right, below the Comment box.

4. Select Tools, Mark (F12) and select Table of Contents. Choose OK to assign this type entry to the First Level. WordPerfect places a [Mark: ToC] code before the comment, and an [End Mark: ToC] code after the comment.

5. Choose Close twice to save the style with your document and return to the main editing screen.

You can use this style over and over to mark table of contents entries. After you define your table of contents and generate it, all the text enclosed in the Contents style appears in the table of contents (see figure 13.2). Note that because the [Mark: ToC] code comes *after* the size and other attributes, the generated table of contents doesn't include these attributes.

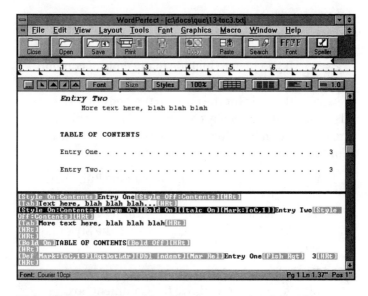

Fig. 13.2 *Sample table of contents entries defined by a style, and the resulting table of contents.*

Change page numbering styles

Suppose you create a long manuscript or a book. You want the preface pages to be numbered in small Roman numerals, but each of the chapters is to begin with Arabic numbers, and each is to start with its own page one. WordPerfect enables you to easily change page number types. Follow these steps:

1. Position the insertion point at the very beginning of the page on which you want the new numbering style to appear.

2. Select **L**ayout, **P**age, Numbering. If page numbering is not turned on, select the page number position you want.

3. From the Number Type pop-up menu, select the numbering style you want (for example, i, ii, iii, iv).

4. Choose OK.

Page numbering now changes to the Roman style, beginning at page i (one). If you need to change to another style, back to the Arabic style for example, repeat the above process, choosing the appropriate Number Type.

Note also that if you intend to use the new page number style in a header or footer, you must insert the Number Type code *preceding* the header or footer code.

Change your document's starting page number

Suppose that you divide a long report you are writing into two sections to make it more manageable for editing. You save the first half as REPORT.1 and the second half as REPORT.2. When you print the files, you want them to be numbered continuously so that the first page of REPORT.2 is actually page 23. Without combining the files, you can change the beginning page number of REPORT.2.

First, open the file in which you want to change the page number (for example, REPORT.2). Then, position the insertion point at the very beginning of the first page. Select **L**ayout, **P**age, Numbering. In the Page Numbering dialog box, make sure the page number **P**osition is selected. In the **N**ew Page Number text box, type the starting number for your document (for example, **23**) and choose OK.

Refer readers to other parts of the document

WordPerfect features an easy-to-use cross-referencing feature that enables you to refer readers to other pages, paragraph numbers, footnotes or endnotes, or to graphic boxes. After you link the current location to the referenced item, WordPerfect adjusts the reference number (for example, the page number) as the document changes.

For example, you want readers to refer to the conclusion of your report. The conclusion is currently on page 4, but if you add more charts or text, the conclusion could end up on page 5 or 6. To establish a cross-reference in which you say "see page xx," follow these steps:

1. Position the insertion point where you want the reference page to appear (for example, right after "see page").

2. Select **Tools, Mark** (F12), and select **Cross-Reference**. WordPerfect displays the Mark Cross-Reference dialog box.

3. You now mark both the reference and the target, and tie the Reference to a Page. If you plan to use the target more than once, type a reference name (for example, **Conclusion**) and choose OK.

4. WordPerfect then instructs you to position the insertion point immediately following the target point (for example, following the Conclusion heading in your report) and press Enter.

5. WordPerfect then places a reference code in your document along with the page number of the target code.

Note: If you change your document, you must use Generate (select **Tools, Generate** or press Alt+F12) to update page reference numbers.

Create a footer that tells readers where they are

One easy way to tell the readers that they are on page x of y total pages is to place a Cross-Reference code in a header or footer, and reference the last page of the document. Follow these steps:

1. At the beginning of the document, create a footer that begins with "Page."

2. Click the Page Numbering button to insert a page number code, and type **of**.

3. Create a cross-reference by selecting **T**ools, Mar**k**(F12), and Cross-**R**eference. Because you are editing a footer, WordPerfect allows you only to mark the Reference. You must type a name (for example, **LASTPAGE**) in the Target Name text box so the footer knows what to refer to. Choose OK.

4. Close the footer editing screen (Ctrl+F4).

5. Position the insertion point at the end of the document.

6. Create the Target reference by pressing Mark Text (F12), selecting Cross-**R**eference, and selecting the Target radio button in the Cross-Reference dialog box. Make sure the Target Name is the same as the one you used in the footer. Choose OK.

You now have to Generate (Alt+F12) before the page reference numbers show up properly, but when you do, your footers should read "Page 1 of 15," "Page 2 of 15," and so on.

Caution: Don't add text *after* the Target reference code or the total page numbers won't be correct.

Use a concordance file for easy indexing

The best long documents have a good index. You can create such an index with very little effort, thanks to WordPerfect's Concordance feature.

As you proofread your document, keep open a separate file into which you copy words that you want to include in the index. You can even create a simple temporary macro to copy words from one document and paste them into the other. After you compile your list of index words (one word per line), sort the index and then remove any duplicate words. Save the resulting file, which becomes your concordance file.

Next, position the insertion point where you want the index to appear. Select Tools, Define (Shift+F12), and select Index. The Define Index dialog box appears. In the Optional Concordance File text box, type the name of the concordance file you created. Choose OK.

Remember that the index won't include any references after the Index definition code, so you should place it at the end of the document.

Finally, generate your document (select Tools, Generate or press Alt+F12). WordPerfect creates an alphabetized index, with page number references, for each of the words included in your concordance file.

Number pages with accompanying text for clear indexes

With documents that change frequently (procedure manuals, parts books), a common practice is to begin each chapter or section at page one so that changes to the document don't require renumbering (and reprinting) the entire document.

The problem is that a comprehensive index can't distinguish between page one in the first chapter and page one in the fifth chapter. However, numbering your pages with accompanying text can help. At the beginning of each chapter, select Layout, Page, Numbering, and then in the Accompanying Text text box, insert "I-","II-", and so on, in front of the ^B character. You need not actually select a page number Position, but could instead have no page numbers or use the page numbering codes in a header or footer.

The separate chapter documents must be included as Subdocuments in a Master document before the Master document index is generated. When it is, the index page numbers reflect the style used in each of the separate chapters (for example, I-5, III-12, etc).

Sort your lists

WordPerfect's Sort feature is flexible, powerful, and easy to use, especially for single-line lists. To sort a list, use Select (F8) to select the entire list. Then choose Tools, Sort and WordPerfect displays the Sort dialog box. If all you want to do is sort the list by the first word on each line, choose OK.

You owe it to yourself to learn more about WordPerfect's Sort feature. For example, in addition to lines, you can sort secondary merge files, paragraphs, and rows in tables. You can sort on any field or combination of fields, and even on specific words within a field. Finally, you can instruct WordPerfect to select certain records before sorting them to give you a sorted subset of your data.

Separate two-word names with a hard space to sort correctly

If you are sorting by the first word in a field, WordPerfect doesn't care what the second word is. Thus, San Gabriel may end up *before* San Diego because, after all, the Sans are sorted properly. To make WordPerfect think that San Diego is just one word, replace the separating space with a hard space by deleting the space and pressing Ctrl+space bar. Do the same with San Gabriel. Sort again and now San Diego appears correctly before San Gabriel.

Replace dash characters with hyphens to sort correctly

WordPerfect is smart enough to know that Johnson-Smith should be sorted by J, even if it is sorting on the last word of "Mary Johnson-Smith." However, if you use a list of names generated by a non-WordPerfect program, such as a database program, the hyphen might actually be a dash character. To check whether you have hyphens or dash characters in your list, open Reveal Codes (Alt+F3). Hyphens appear in brackets ([-]).

When WordPerfect sorts words separated by the dash character, it sorts on the words separately. Thus, Mary Johnson-Smith would be listed *after* Ronald Peterson. To remedy this problem, replace (Ctrl+F2) all of the dash characters (Ctrl+ -) with a hyphen (-), and then sort the list.

Change sort fields when you sort paragraphs with hanging indents

A common use for sorting, especially in academics, is to alphabetize bibliographic entries. A typical entry begins with a hanging indent, which actually is an Indent code followed by a Margin Release code.

When you instruct WordPerfect to sort by paragraphs, as you would in this case, no sorting takes place, or if it does, the sort is incorrect. The problem lies in the field on which you are sorting.

WordPerfect separates fields by tabs, indent codes, or margin release codes. Thus, the author's last name is actually the *third* field in the paragraph. Change the sort keys to sort on field 3 and the sort will turn out the way you expect it to.

Use automatic footnote/endnote numbering

WordPerfect can keep track of the order of your footnotes, and reserve the proper space for them at the bottom of each page. As you add or delete footnotes, WordPerfect readjusts the numbering sequence so that your footnotes never are out of order.

To use footnotes (or endnotes), position the insertion point where you want your footnote to appear and select Layout, Page, Footnote, Create. In the footnote editing screen, enter the text of your footnote and then select Close (Ctrl+F4) to return to your document.

Note: Remember that footnotes print in the Document Initial Font. Check Layout, Document, Initial Font to make sure it matches the font you are using for the body of your text.

Converting footnotes to endnotes

Footnotes are much easier for readers to deal with than are endnotes. Publishers, however, would rather work with a list of endnotes (footnotes that are listed at the end of the document). If you must change footnotes to endnotes, you can use two different methods.

The first method is to use the FOOTEND macro that comes with WordPerfect. If you have many notes, this method may take quite a bit of time. A much quicker method, especially if you have many notes, is to define and turn on newspaper-style columns at the beginning of the document, then delete the column codes. Because footnotes are not permitted in columns, WordPerfect converts them all to endnotes.

Finally, if you need to convert endnotes to footnotes, you can use the ENDFOOT macro that comes with WordPerfect.

Divide your large documents into several smaller ones

If the size of your document begins to get out of hand, or you find yourself working with several chapters in a large project, divide the large document into several smaller ones for easier editing and navigation.

WordPerfect's Master and Subdocument feature makes this division a breeze. First create the Master document. Include the Document Initial codes and Document Initial Font you intend to use for the entire document. Also include the definitions and locations for the table of contents, indexes, and other lists.

Finally, add the Subdocuments. Position the insertion point where you want the subdocument to appear (for example, Chapter 1), and then select Tools, Master Document, Subdocument. The Include Subdocument dialog box appears (nearly identical to the Open File dialog box). Select the file you want to include as a Subdocument. WordPerfect places a Subdocument code in the Master document, including the name and path of the filename.

After you finish including all of the subdocuments (and save your Master document), you then can generate the Master document. The table of contents, index, and lists are based on all the subdocuments as well as the Master document itself.

Unless you specifically change the page numbering or footnote numbering sequence, WordPerfect automatically updates all such numbers across all the subdocuments (for example, pages 1 through 99, footnotes 1 through 72, etc.).

14

CHAPTER

Using Numbered Lists, Numbered Paragraphs, and Outlines

Word processing users seem to have forgotten that the computer has a tremendous ability to calculate and manipulate numbers. Instead, they type, and retype numbers when the computer can do that for them. This chapter focuses on those number-related things that WordPerfect can do so well: dates, numbered lists and paragraphs, outlines, and math calculations.

Use Date Code for revision dates

Do you have documents that need periodic revising? WordPerfect can automatically change the revision date if you use the Date Code feature. Select Tools, Date, Code (Ctrl+Shift+F5) and WordPerfect inserts a code that reads the computer's current date and displays it on-screen. If you save the document and open it tomorrow, tomorrow's date appears on-screen.

Caution: Don't use the Date Code for date-sensitive or legal documents in which you don't want the date to change. Use Date Text (Ctrl+F5) instead.

Let WordPerfect number your lists

How many times have you had to renumber a list because you forgot to include an item, or decided later to delete one? If you use WordPerfect for Windows' automatic paragraph numbering when you create the list, you can have WordPerfect renumber the list for you. Follow these steps:

1. At the top of the document, or in Document Initial Codes, select Tools, Outline, Define (Alt+Shift+F5). WordPerfect displays the Define Paragraph Numbering dialog box.

2. From the pop-up lists of Predefined Formats, select Paragraph and note the numbering style: 1., a., i., (1), and so on.

3. Deselect the Outline On check box and choose OK.

4. Instead of typing the numbers for your list, press Paragraph Number (Alt+F5), press Enter, and press Tab or indent.

5. Type the text for the list item. Repeat steps 4 and 5 until all the items in the list are entered.

WordPerfect generates each item's number automatically. If you later insert an item, each subsequent number automatically increases to reflect the addition. If you delete an item, each number decreases. If you change the order of the items, each number changes to reflect the change in sequence. The [Par Num:Auto] code remains constant, however.

Create a macro to insert paragraph numbers

Because you plan to use the automatic paragraph numbering feature a lot more now, how about an easier way to insert paragraph numbers? Instead of pressing Alt+F5 and Enter, create a simple macro to do the same thing—for example, Ctrl+A (**A**utomatic Numbering) (see Chapter 4). In addition, you can have the macro automatically add an Indent code after the paragraph number. You also can add this macro to your favorite Button Bar (see Chapter 5).

Use your paragraph numbering macro to create outlines

 WordPerfect's Outlining feature is powerful and flexible; however, most users find the feature difficult to learn and to use. Essentially, the Outlining feature uses the [Par Num:Auto] code for each outline number. The number of tabs before the code establishes the outline level and determines what number WordPerfect displays. The left margin is the first level, the first tab stop after that is the second level, the next tab stop the third level, and so on (see fig. 14.1).

Instead of turning on WordPerfect's Outline feature, use your Paragraph Numbering macro to create outlines. Assuming that you made your macro Ctrl+A, follow these steps:

1. At the left margin, press Ctrl+A and type the text of the first Level One entry.

2. Press Enter. If the next item is also at Level One, press Ctrl+A again. If the item is a Level Two item, however, press Tab before pressing Ctrl+A.

3. Continue by using tabs to position the insertion point at the level you want and then pressing Ctrl+A to insert the appropriate paragraph number.

Note: If you need to adjust a line to a different level, insert or delete tabs until the paragraph number lines up where you want it. The outline number adjusts automatically.

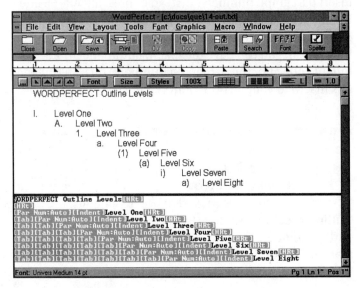

Fig. 14.1 *WordPerfect's outlining levels.*

Use Outlining to move your families

WordPerfect can adjust outlines by moving whole families (outline sections, including all of its subsections) up, down, left, or right. Although you may not want to learn or use the Outlining feature to create the outline, you can turn outlining on after the fact and use some of its features to adjust outlines you create with your paragraph numbering macro.

You can move whole families of your outline by following these steps:

1. If outline is not already turned on (check the Status Bar), position the insertion point immediately

preceding the beginning of the outline. Then choose Tools, Outline, Define (Alt+Shift+F5). In the Options group, deselect the Enter Inserts Paragraph check box, and press Enter.

2. Move the insertion point to the family (section) you want to move and choose Tools, Outline, Move Family. WordPerfect highlights the entire family.

3. Press the up- or down-arrow keys to change the order of the family.

4. Press the right- or left-arrow keys to promote or demote the family to a different level.

5. When the family is positioned as you want, press Enter.

Define multiple outlines in the same document

If you create an outline in one part of your document, then attempt to create a second one later, WordPerfect continues numbering the second outline where the first outline left off. If you want to include chunks of narrative text between outline sections, this feature is useful. However, if you want two separate outlines, you must define the second outline:

1. Move the insertion point to the beginning of the second outline. Then choose Tools, Outline, Define (Alt+Shift+F5). Note that the Outline Define dialog box displays the number 1 in the Starting Outline Number text box.

2. Deselect the Outline On and Enter Inserts Paragraph Number boxes.

3. Choose OK. Your outline now starts again at number 1.

Change the outline numbering style

By default, WordPerfect uses the outlining style of numbers (I., A., 1., etc.), but you also can select the paragraph style (1., a., i., etc.), the legal style (1., 1.1., 1.1.1., etc.), or even a bullet style that uses no numbers. Choose **Tools, Outline, Define**; then from the Predefined Formats pop-up list, choose the style you want to use.

If you don't like any of the predefined styles, you can select a different numbering sequence, or you can create an entirely unique style. To change Level I to Level A, for example, choose **User-defined** from the Predefined Formats pop-up list, choose Level 1, and change Style to A.

Use predefined styles when formatting outlines

One of the advantages to using the regular WordPerfect Outlining feature is that you can use special styles to format your outline. For example, you can align all of your paragraph numbers on the decimal by using the Right Par (right-aligned paragraph) style.

To turn on outlining and use a predefined style, first choose **Tools, Outline, Define** (Alt+Shift+F5). WordPerfect displays the Define Paragraph Numbering dialog box, in which you choose **Change** (style). WordPerfect then displays the Outline Styles dialog box. Select a style and choose **Select**; then return to your document by choosing OK.

Create a numberless outline with styles

If you don't like the outline styles offered by WordPerfect, you can create your own. Customized outline styles enable you to quickly create outlines where the text of one level is formatted differently than the text of another level.

For example, you can make the first level items bold and large and put the third level items in italics (see fig. 14.2). You also can choose not to include paragraph numbers at all, but let the style indicate the outline level.

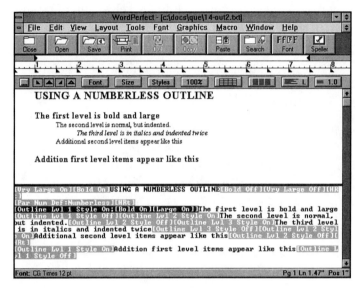

Fig. 14.2 *A numberless outline with styles.*

To create a unique outline style, follow these steps:

1. Select Tools, Outline, Define (Alt+Shift+F5).

2. Select Change Style.

3. In the Outline Styles dialog box, choose Create. WordPerfect displays the Edit Outline Style dialog box.

4. Type a short name in the Name text box and a longer description in the Description text box.

5. For each of the levels you want to define, you must specify whether this style is an open or a paired style.

Choose Paired to have the style automatically turn off the style features at the end of the text for that level.

6. If you want WordPerfect to close a style and open the next style when you press Enter, select Enter Key and select Style Off/On from the pop-up list.

7. Click Level 1, and select Edit. WordPerfect displays the Style Editor. Place the beginning codes before the Comment, and any closing codes after the Comment.

8. Choose Close (Ctrl+F4) to close the Style Editor and return to the Outline Styles dialog box. Repeat steps 7 and 8 for the remaining levels, adding the appropriate number of indent codes before the Comment.

9. In the Define Outline Styles dialog box, choose OK.

10. In the Outline Styles dialog box, choose Save As and type a unique name for your outline style and choose OK. You can now choose this style to use with outlines in any document.

Use simple math in tables

WordPerfect enables you to add, subtract, multiply, and divide numbers, but only within tables. You must first create a table; then place formulas in the appropriate cells.

To create a formula, position the insertion point in the cell where you want the formula, and then select Layout, Tables, Formula. In the Formula text box, type the formula you want. For example, to add the rows above the current cell, type +. To multiply a subtotal in cell B4 by a 5.5% tax rate, for example, type B4*.055.

15

Using Macros and Keyboards

Covering both macros and keyboards in one chapter of a short book of tips is like covering a house with a teaspoon of paint: it can't be done. Instead, the focus of this chapter is to offer a few nifty ideas and provide a little motivation for you to try these powerful features for yourself.

Get help from the *Macro Manual* and Macro Help

You're ready to write your first macro, but you're not sure where to start. You open the WordPerfect Reference and find information on recording and playing a macro, but virtually nothing is provided on programming macros. Fortunately, two additional sources for getting help on macros exist.

The first source is the *Macro Manual.* Soon after the initial release of WordPerfect for Windows, WordPerfect Corporation published *WordPerfect for Windows Macros Manual,* which includes a thorough description (more than 500 pages) of WordPerfect for Windows' macro procedures and commands. You can obtain the manual from your local retailer or directly from WordPerfect Corporation.

The second source is WordPerfect's On-Line Help for Macros. When you install WordPerfect for Windows, you have the choice to install the Macro On-Line help also. If you choose to do so, a new menu item, Using Macros, appears on the Help menu. To access this file, choose Help, Using Macros.

Macro Help provides alphabetically listed help screens for each macro command, including details on the purpose and function of the command, a listing of the proper syntax, descriptions of any parameters, and often related commands to which you can refer simply by clicking the topic. Many sections include a ShowMe! button that offers a short example of how the command is used.

If you are new to programming macros, Macro Help also offers brief tutorials on macro procedures, including the powerful and useful Macro Dialog commands.

Finally, in Macro Help, you can also find a description of the macros that ship with WordPerfect.

Access Macro Help quickly when writing macros

While writing macros, especially at first, you spend a great deal of time going to the Macro Help screen. However, to minimize the waiting time you encounter when switching back and forth, don't close the help screen when you are through. Instead, for quicker access from WordPerfect to the Macro Help screen, select Macro Help as you normally do (choose Help, Using Macros), and then press Alt+Tab to switch back and forth between Macro Help and WordPerfect for Windows.

Copy and run ShowMe! macros

The Macro Help screens often contain ShowMe! examples, which are working macros. While in Macro Help, choose Edit, Copy. In the Copy dialog box, select the text you want to copy and choose the Copy button. Then, switch back to WordPerfect (Alt+Tab). In a blank screen, select Edit, Paste (or press Shift+Insert). If necessary, make other editing changes and save as a *.WCM macro in your macro directory. When you play it, you see how the sample macro actually works. If you don't want to keep the macro (you probably won't), delete it.

Cause recorded macros to pause when played

Normally, when you record a dialog box action in a macro, the results of the action are played back—not the action itself. For example, if you set new margins, those margin settings are placed in the document when you play the macro. You are not provided with the opportunity to change those settings.

When recording your macro, however, notice the small, empty box that appears at the upper-right corner of many dialog boxes. If you click this box (see fig. 15.1), the macro pauses when you play it, allowing you to modify the settings in the dialog box.

Fig. 15.1 *Clicking the Record Marker while recording a macro.*

For the macro to suggest certain default settings, record the dialog box with the suggested settings, but do not click the Record Marker box. Then record the dialog box again, this time clicking the Record Marker box. When you play the macro, WordPerfect actually inserts your recorded default settings codes, and because of Autocode placement, the macro then replaces them with the changes you specify.

Add the Windows calculator to WordPerfect

A handy, perhaps necessary tool that WordPerfect doesn't have is a calculator. Fortunately, you can call up the Windows calculator with a macro. Type the following:

```
Application (WP;WPWP;Default;"WPWPUS.WCD")

AppExecute("calc.exe")
```

(The AppExecute command works with any Windows or DOS program.)

Save the macro in your macros directory as CALC.WCM. For even more convenience, you can name it CTRLSFTC.WCM and thus execute it by pressing Ctrl+Shift+C. As noted elsewhere, you also can assign the macro to one of your menus or Button Bars.

Add macros to your menus

One method of placing macros in a menu is to select Macro, Assign to Menu. But another, more intriguing way is to create a macro that actually modifies your WordPerfect menus to include macros and menu descriptions of your own choosing. Suppose you want to add to your Tools Menu the macro that calls up the Windows calculator. You search the Tools Menu and find that all the good menu letters are taken (such as C or L). You then decide to make the menu entry Zippy Calculator.

You open a blank screen and type the following macro,
saving it to your macros directory:

```
Application (WP;WPWP;Default;"WPWPUS.WCD")

MenuAddItem

(

      MenuName:"Tools Menu";

      ItemName:"Calculator";

      Offset:21;

      Type:0;

      ItemText:"&Zippy Calculator";

      MacroName:"c:\wpwin\macros\calc.wcm";

      Prompt:"Start up the Windows Calculator"

)
```

Menuname is the name of the menu listing where you plan to
assign the macro. ItemName is a variable of your choosing.
Offset is how far down the menu the item will appear.
(Count menu items as well as separator lines.) Type is 0 for
a macro, 1 for a separator line, and 2 for a submenu.
ItemText is your own menu description (the & sign makes
the letter that follows it the underlined hot key). Prompt is
the text that appears on the status bar when the mouse
points to the menu item.

You must run this macro each time you use WordPerfect
because the menu items you add don't remain on the
menus when you exit. You might consider adding this
procedure to a startup macro that you run each time you
start WordPerfect.

Create your own dialog boxes

When you begin to write, rather than simply record, your
own macros, you soon find that the macro-command

language's capability to handle user input is severely limited. For example, you have to get input from the user one item at a time.

One of the more exciting additions to WordPerfect for Windows is the Macro Dialog language, which enables you to create dialog boxes for obtaining user input. At any one time, these boxes can contain several methods of gathering information from the user, and the command language is enhanced so that it can analyze and take advantage of the data it collects.

Macro Dialog commands can't be described and covered here, but you can use the on-line help screens to learn more about them (neither the WordPerfect Reference nor the Macro Manual includes anything about these commands). Try a few ShowMe! examples before creating your own custom dialog boxes.

Use shortcut names for macros

A quick and easy way to play macros is to name them CTRLx or CTRLSFTx, where x is a single letter or number. For example, if you want a quick way to play the macro that brings up the Windows Calculator program, name the macro CTRLSFTC.WCM. By pressing Ctrl+Shift+C, you accomplish the same thing as pressing Macro Play (Alt+F10) and entering the macro name.

Although Ctrl+Shift+x macros involve one more key to press than the simple Ctrl+x macros, finding an available key to assign may be easier because many of the Ctrl+x keys already are assigned to CUA keyboard functions. For example, Ctrl+C is the Copy function but Ctrl+Shift+C is not assigned.

To assign CTRL and CTRLSFT names when you record a macro, press Ctrl or Ctrl+Shift and the letter you want to assign when asked for the macro name.

To assign CTRL and CTRLSFT names when you write a macro, save the macro using those names plus the letter you want to assign.

If you already have a macro that you saved with a different name, press Macro Play (Alt+F10), select the macro name you want to change (but don't play it), and then choose Options, Move/Rename. In the To text box of the Move/Rename File dialog box, type the new name (for example, CTRLSFTC.WCM) and choose Move.

Use a temporary macro for ad hoc tasks

 A temporary macro makes sense for tasks that you need for the moment but may never need again. Suppose you have to change the format of a report that lists people's names in a first/last order; instead, you need the names listed in a last/first order. Your macro to search, select, cut, and paste is one that you probably will never need again, so you assign it a macro name that you reserve just for temporary macros.

This type of macro is actually the same as any other macro, but the name you use for it gets recycled the next time you record a temporary macro. By using the same name for your temporary macros, you don't have to worry about deleting old and unused macros.

The name you use for your temporary macros is not important, but being able to remember it and use it easily is. For example, Ctrl+0 (zero) is a good candidate for your temporary macro name.

If, after recording and using a temporary macro, you decide you want to keep it, just rename it so it won't get replaced by your next temporary macro!

Repeat macros with this handy macro

 Temporary macros often perform a specific task—such as modifying the organization of one line in a database report—but then are needed again in the next line. You don't want to go to the trouble of programming the macro itself so that it repeats. Instead, you can use the following macro to specify the macro you want to repeat and then let this macro repeater do the work for you.

The following macro also is an example of the use of macro dialog box commands. When you run the macro, it first cautions you about not being able to work with uncompiled macros. If you choose OK to proceed, the macro prompts you for the number of times you want to repeat a macro and asks you the name of the macro (see fig. 15.2). When you choose OK, it repeats the macro you specify the number of times you indicate.

Note: If the macro that is repeated executes a Quit command, the macro doing the repeating will stop.

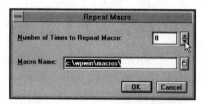

Fig. 15.2 *The Repeat Macro dialog box, created with macro dialog commands.*

A macro to repeat another compiled macro:

```
Application (WP;WPWP;Default;"WPWPUS.WCD")
OnCancel(Quit@)
OnError(Quit@)
Caution:=500
```

```
DialogDefine(Caution;50;50;200;100;1+2+16+512;"Caution")
DialogAddText(Caution;50;10;20;180;40;1;"CAUTION: This
    macro repeats compiled macros only.  Your macro must
    have been run at least once, or compiled, before using
    this macro repeater.")
DialogDisplay(Caution;1)
If(MacroDialogResult=2) Go(Quit@) Endif
DialogDestroy(Caution)
Repeater:=1000
DialogDefine(Repeater;50;50;200;100;1+2+16+512;"Repeat
    Macro")
DialogAddText(Repeater;50;5;13;150;12;1;"&Number of Times
    to Repeat Macro:")
Counter:=8
DialogAddCounter(Repeater;51;150;10;40;15;0;Counter;1;10000
    ;1)
DialogAddText(Repeater;60;5;40;150;12;1;"&Macro Name:")
GetWPData(MacroPath;MacroPath!)
FileName:=MacroPath
DialogAddFileNameBox(Repeater;61;55;38;135;15;0;FileName;
    MacroPath;"*.wcm")
DialogDisplay(Repeater;61)
If(MacroDialogResult=2) Go(Quit@) Endif
StrPos(Place;"\";FileName)
If(Place=0)
    FullFileName:=MacroPath+FileName
    Else FullFileName:=FileName
EndIf
For(RepeatIt;1;RepeatIt<=Counter;RepeatIt+1)
Run(FullFileName)
EndFor
Label(Quit@)
Quit
```

Note: The above listing is formatted for easier reading.
However, you can just type the hanging indent paragraphs
as regular paragraphs without the indents. Type the
macro in a new file and save it in your macros directory
as MACAGAIN.WCM (or whatever name you choose). If
you find it useful, you can assign it to your menu or to a
Button Bar.

Use the Command Inserter to aid in writing macros

At some point, you need to write, rather than record, macros. Typing the commands, even when you know them, can be tedious. Fortunately, WordPerfect's Macro Command Inserter comes to the rescue.

To activate the Macro Command Inserter, press Ctrl+M. By default, the Macro Command Inserter dialog box lists the macro programming commands and the proper syntax for each command. If you select WP from the Type pop-up list, the Command Inserter lists WordPerfect feature commands along with any applicable parameters and members. Use the cursor or scroll bar to find the command you want, and then press Enter or double-click the command to enter it into the Token Edit box. In this box, you can add any additional information required by the command syntax. Choose Insert to place the command in your macro document. You can leave the dialog box on-screen for future use or choose Close to clear it.

Customize your keyboard

Keyboards, menus, and macros all go hand in hand to make working with WordPerfect easier and more efficient. Any macro that you find particularly useful can be assigned to one of your keyboard keys. In addition, if you find a menu item that is buried deep in the menu structure but that you use often, you can assign it to a key that you don't use very often. Finally, you also can assign text or WordPerfect commands to any key.

Suppose, for example, you use the numeric keypad for cursor movement (a good idea). If you assign the Select function to the number 5 key, your hand is in position to Select with the number 5 key and move the cursor with the other fingers. This arrangement makes for one-handed selecting of text with the keyboard—almost like using a mouse!

Use caution when making keyboard changes

You should use caution when making changes to your keyboard. If you make too many changes, you can disable needed keystrokes and confuse yourself or others who use your computer.

In addition, while assigning macros to your keyboard can speed performance, it makes accidentally playing such macros easier, too. Only assign to your keyboards macros that don't exhibit destructive behavior.

Remember, you can always return to your default CUA keyboard by choosing File, Preferences, Keyboard, Default (CUA) and then choosing OK.

Compile your macros before assigning them to a keyboard

Uncompiled macros cannot be assigned to a keyboard. WordPerfect displays an error message when you try to do so. Play the macro once (Alt+F10) to automatically compile it.

16

Merging

Learning to manipulate your data by merging from one
file, or even from the keyboard, to another file not only
can save you time, but also really can be fun. This chapter gives a few tips on WordPerfect's Merge feature.

Use the Merge Button Bar

The merge commands are buried rather deeply in
the menu system except for the basic {END FIELD}
(Alt+Enter) and {END RECORD} (Alt+Shift+Enter) codes.

The Merge Button Bar, however, places most merge
commands at your immediate disposal (see figure 16.1).
Use QuickMenu by clicking the secondary (right)
mouse button while the pointer is over the current Button Bar. From the list of available Button Bars, select
MERGE.WWB.

Fig. 16.1 *The Merge Button Bar.*

Design a functional secondary file

The secondary file that contains your merge data is much more important than the primary files that use it. You can modify a primary file until it works properly, but a poorly designed secondary file is harder to fix.

When you first decide to create a secondary file of data, consider carefully just what information you're going to need and how you intend to use that information. For example, although WordPerfect permits you to create several lines in one record, you will be quite limited in what you can do with an address unless you place the street number, city, state, and zip code in separate fields.

Remember that you can use the same data in many different primary forms including letters, mailing labels, name tags, greeting cards, invoices, and so on. Make sure your secondary file is flexible enough to meet all these needs.

Use field names to make data entry easier

As you type a secondary merge file, the status bar shows the current field number you are typing. For very simple secondary files this notification is adequate, but if you have several fields, keeping track of which field contains what information is difficult.

However, if you assign names to your fields, the name of the field appears on the status bar as you enter data, thus prompting you for the data you need for that field.

When you get ready to use the data in a primary form, you also can use field names rather than numbers. To add field names, first position the insertion point at the very top of your secondary merge file, and then select the Mrg Code button on the Button Bar, or select Tools, Merge, Merge Codes. From the list, select Field Names.

Use a consistent naming scheme for your merge files

Identify your primary and secondary merge files by using file name extensions that reflect the type of document they are. For example, if you name all of your primary files using the .PF extension and your secondary files using the .SF extension, you can easily find and use them. You can even set up Quick Lists for each (.PF and .SF) type of file, to make finding and using your primary and secondary files even easier.

Get rid of the Field prompt

If you accidentally press Alt+Enter, WordPerfect dutifully places an {END FIELD} code in your document. You backspace to erase it, but the Field: 1 prompt still appears on the status bar. To get rid of it, press Ctrl+Home to go to the top of your document. The message now is gone, and you can press Ctrl+G and choose Last Position to return to where you were working.

Use database files instead of WordPerfect secondary merge files

If your company keeps its data in a regular database program, you still can use that data in WordPerfect merges.

First, ask the person that manages the database to export an ASCII file of the data. The file typically uses common characters such as quote marks and commas to delimit the fields and records of the database:

```
"Mary Jones","123 Fourth  Street","Belmont","CA","91111"
```

To use such a file in place of a secondary merge file, begin your merge as you normally do, but select the ASCII delimited text (DOS) check box. WordPerfect then displays the Text File Delimiters dialog box. Indicate what characters or codes are used by the ASCII file to separate the fields, and what are used to separate each record. For example, for the preceding record, a quote mark (") begins each field, a quote and comma (",) ends each field, and a quote and hard return (")CR) ends each record.

Caution: Do not open the ASCII data file and save it in WordPerfect format or this method will not work.

If you often merge using the same field delimiters, you can set these permanently by selecting File, Preferences, Merge.

Customize your merges with {IF BLANK} and {IF NOT BLANK} merge codes

Secondary merge files must contain the same number of fields per record, even if the fields contain no information. When you merge to a primary document, such fields may cause empty lines to appear in the merged result. You can use the {IF BLANK} and {IF NOT BLANK} merge codes to customize the way WordPerfect uses the blank fields. Consider, for example, the primary form in figure 16.2.

Note that the {IF NOT BLANK} statement places the Phone field *and* a hard return if the field is not blank. WordPerfect omits the extra hard return if the field is blank.

Note also that punctuation (such as spaces between sentences) has to account for records that have information as well as those that don't. And finally, don't forget that every IF code must have a corresponding {END IF} code.

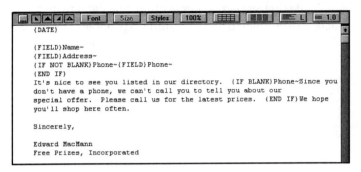

```
(DATE)

(FIELD)Name~
(FIELD)Address~
(IF NOT BLANK)Phone~(FIELD)Phone~
(END IF)
It's nice to see you listed in our directory.  (IF BLANK)Phone~Since you
don't have a phone, we can't call you to tell you about our
special offer.  Please call us for the latest prices.  (END IF)We hope
you'll shop here often.

Sincerely,

Edward MacMann
Free Prizes, Incorporated
```

Fig. 16.2 *A primary form that uses {IF BLANK} and {IF NOT BLANK} codes.*

Use Merge to create memos

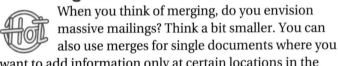 When you think of merging, do you envision massive mailings? Think a bit smaller. You can also use merges for single documents where you want to add information only at certain locations in the document. Using Merge saves searching for the text entry locations.

For example, you can use Merge for an office memo. When you type a memo, you include a letter head, date, TO: and FROM: lines, and so on. If you create a template memo form, you have to open the form and move the insertion point to the TO: and SUBJECT: lines before typing the information that goes there. You also have to remember to save the file using a new name.

To automate this process, place {INPUT} merge commands where you need to type the variable data. Use this new file as a primary file in a merge, even though there is no secondary file, and WPWin will automatically stop at each command to allow you to enter the data. To move to the next {INPUT} command, press Alt+Enter.

Finally, if you use such a merge often, you can create a macro to automate the merge start up process.

17

CHAPTER

Managing Files

Good file management practices involve being able to store and then locate your documents as quickly and efficiently as possible. Of course, you can add good backup practices to this list as well. This chapter includes tips on managing your documents and using WordPerfect, WordPerfect's File Manager, and even DOS.

Get organized

Planning the organization of your hard disk files is no different than planning how you will file documents in a file drawer. Get a yellow pad and make a sketch of how your files are organized.

Most people would never throw all their documents into one folder and toss that folder into a file drawer. Likewise, you don't want to store all your documents in the same place you keep your WordPerfect program files, your graphics files, and your macros. Make sure all these files are kept in separate directories.

To find out how organized you are, start by selecting File, Preferences, Location of Files. The listing that appears should indicate where you keep your documents, graphics, printer drivers, macros, dictionaries, and program files. If any of the entries are blank, make a note of it on your scratch pad.

To find out how your entire hard disk is organized, use the File Manager's Navigator. Choose File, File Manager. If the Navigator is not one of the windows you see when the File Manager starts, press Ctrl+N or choose View, WP File Navigator (see fig. 17.1). At the very least, the Navigator displays the drives you have at your disposal. Double-click your hard disk drive (for example, -c-). In the next window, the Navigator displays the files and directories contained in the root directory. Begin sketching an upside-down tree of your directories only. Next, double-click each directory and note any additional subdirectories until you have sketched your entire tree.

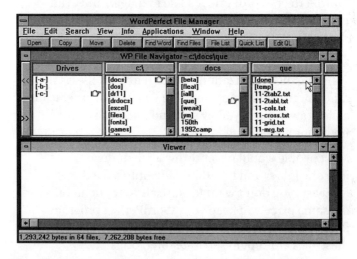

Fig. 17.1 *Using the Navigator in WordPerfect's File Manager.*

Using that tree as a guide, determine where you want to store your documents or any other file locations that were not listed when you chose Preferences, Location of Files.

Finally, from the File Manager, press Ctrl+T or choose File, Create a Directory. In the Create Directory dialog box, type the location, including the entire path, of any directories you need but don't have. For example, if you plan to store your documents as a subdirectory of the WPWIN directory, you type **C:\WPWIN\DOCS**.

Get a quicker tree

DOS also comes with a TREE program that lists your directories for you. If you use DOS version 4.0 or later, the program displays your directories graphically.

Minimize WordPerfect, and start up the DOS prompt icon from the Windows Program Manager. This action takes you to a DOS prompt (C:\WINDOWS>). Type **TREE C:\ > C:\WPWIN\DOCS\MYTREE.LST**. If your documents are stored somewhere else, type that location instead. When you press Enter, this DOS program generates a listing of your hard disk structure and directs the output to the file you list (for example, MYTREE.LST). When you get the DOS prompt again, enter **EXIT** to return to Windows.

Finally, maximize WordPerfect, and then open the file you just generated (for example, MYTREE.LST). Because the listing is an ASCII file, WordPerfect displays the Convert File Format dialog box. Press Enter to convert the file to the WordPerfect format. You now can examine, add comments to, or print the tree listing of your hard disk.

Move your files

If you need to change the location of a file, press Open (F4) and browse until you find the file you want to move. Select the file (but don't open it) and choose Option,

Move/Rename. In the Move/Rename dialog box, type the new location (just the path name, not the file name).

The effect of moving a file is the same as copying to the new location and deleting at the old location. Moving, obviously, is much quicker because you are actually just renaming the location.

If you need to move several files, use the File Manager (File, File Manager), which enables you to select more than one file at a time. For example, from a list of files, you can click and drag the mouse to select several files in a row or you can hold down the Ctrl key and click individual files until you have the ones you want. Then, press Ctrl+R or choose File, Move/Rename and specify the new location.

Use the mouse to copy or move files in the File Manager

If you have at least two file list windows open in the File Manager, you can copy or move files from one window to another by selecting the files you want to copy and then using the mouse to drag those files to the other window.

To move a file, first select it with the mouse; then hold down the primary (left) mouse button and drag the file *sideways* to the appropriate file listing (the mouse pointer changes to a "MOVE" icon). You copy files the same way, but you have to press and hold down the Ctrl key before moving the mouse.

Leave Change Default Dir unchecked to avoid misplacing files

In file listing dialog boxes, such as Open File or Save As, a small check box sits at the lower left inviting you to click it. *Don't.* With the box checked, if you change to another directory, that new directory becomes the default directory for opening and saving files. Remembering to change your default directory back to its normal location takes a conscious effort. When you forget to do so, new files you create are saved by default in a location other than what you expect.

If you indeed plan to spend a lot of time in a directory other than your normal documents directory, go ahead and choose Change Default Dir. Just remember to change the default directory back to your documents directory and then deselect the box before you exit WordPerfect.

Make navigating easier with Quick List

WordPerfect's Quick List feature makes quickly displaying a listing of commonly used directories or files simple. If you select the Quick List check box in any file listing dialog box, you see a short list of descriptive names (for example, Graphics Files). If you double-click any of these names, the left side of the dialog box displays the files found in that location.

Select Edit Quick List to add or delete entries in your Quick List. You even can add a single file or a subgroup of files to your Quick List. For example, suppose you are working on a long report, FINAL.RPT, that you need to come back to often. You could add a "Report Project" Quick List entry that includes only the file FINAL.RPT. Then, by double-clicking Report Project in the Quick List, the file list displays just that file.

If for some reason you need to see the actual directories and structure of your hard disk, deselect Quick List, and WordPerfect displays your directories. Remember that the [. .] directory is the *parent*, or directory above your current directory. The [name] directories are *subdirectories*, or below the current directory.

See when a file was last updated

Sometimes you need to know when a file was last updated (time and date) and perhaps what size it is. Press Open (F4), locate the appropriate file, and click it once (do not open it). In the upper part of the dialog box, WordPerfect lists File Info, including number of bytes (size) and the date and time it was last saved.

Find files quickly

When you select File, Find Files, WordPerfect displays a dialog box that enables you to search for a file by file name or file pattern (for example, REPORT.*). You also can search for files based on the words they contain. You can search the entire disk drive or the current directory (with or without subdirectories). This method may take several minutes, but it is probably quicker than the method you now use.

Use QuickFinder for warp speed file finding

 Although using Find Files is a speedy way to locate files, you can reduce the search from minutes to seconds by using WordPerfect's QuickFinder.

Before you can use QuickFinder, you have to create a QuickFinder index. To create this index, you must start the QuickFinder File Indexer program, which is separate from WordPerfect. Go to the Windows Program Manager and double-click the QuickFinder File Indexer; then follow these steps to create a new index:

1. Choose Create. The Create Index Name dialog box appears. Type the descriptive name you want to give your index, and Choose OK.

2. Next, in the Add Directory or File text box, type the full name of the directory you want to index. You also can indicate a file or a set of files (for example, C:\DOCS*.RPT). To include subdirectories of the location you indicate, choose the Include Subtree check box.

3. Choose Add to place the location in the Directories to Index list.

4. Repeat steps 2 and 3 until you have included all the files or directories you want to index. Then, choose Index.

The QuickFinder File Indexer searches each of the files in the set, indexes every word in them, and signals when it is finished.

You now can use the QuickFinder index when you use Find Files in WordPerfect. Choose the QuickFinder Index radio button and specify the word or words you want to find; then, when you choose Find, you get a nearly instantaneous list of files that contains the word for which you are searching.

Update your QuickFinder indexes regularly

You should use the QuickFinder File Indexer to update your indexes at least weekly. This way, when you need to find something quickly, you don't have to wait around while the QuickFinder File Indexer reindexes the new files you have added.

To access the QuickFinder File Indexer more easily, WordPerfect provides a macro that starts the Indexer from within WordPerfect. Press Macro Play (Alt+F10) and play QFINDEX.WCM, or assign this macro to your File menu by playing the following macro:

```
Application (WP;WPWP;Default;"WPWPUS.WCD")
MenuAddItem
(
    MenuName:"File Menu";
    ItemName:"QFind";
    Offset:11;
    Type:0;
    ItemText:"QuickFind &Indexer";
    MacroName:"c:\wpwin\macros\qfindex.wcm";
    Prompt:"Start up the QuickFinder File Indexer
Program"
)
```

If you make this macro part of a startup macro, it appears
to be part of your regular WordPerfect Program, and you
won't have any excuse for not using it.

Search for words in the File Viewer

When you are in any of the File Lists (for example, Open
File) or in the File Manager, you can view the currently
selected file. You also can search for words in the Viewer.
After choosing View, click anywhere on the View window;
then press Search (F2). The Viewer Search dialog box ap-
pears. In the Find text box, type the word or partial word
for which you are looking. You can use Match Whole Word
Only, or you can find a word that is part of a larger word.
When you choose Search, WordPerfect advances until it
finds the word. To continue the search, choose Search
Next from the dialog control menu or press Search Next
(Shift+F2).

Place your backup files in a separate directory

If you use WordPerfect's Original Document Backup option, every time you save a file on which you are working,
WordPerfect saves a backup copy of it. The files, which
end in *.BK!, eventually use a lot of disk space. To make
deleting unneeded backup files easier, store them in an

entirely separate directory (for example, C:\BACK).
Choose File, Preferences, Location of files and specify the
new location in the Backup Files text box.

Note: You may first need to use the File Manager to
create the backup directory you specify.

When you decide to delete old backup files, you can
choose File Manager, Search, Advanced Find and specify
the date range you want to delete (for example, 11/01/92
to 02/01/93). Then, press Ctrl+S (Edit, Select All) to select
all the files and Ctrl+D (File, Delete) to delete them all. The
File Manager deletes only files saved during that three
month period.

Make separate backup copies by date

Using WordPerfect's File Manager, you can copy files by
date from your hard disk to a floppy disk for archiving.
Suppose that you want a second copy on floppy disk of
everything you created since last week. Follow these steps:

1. Start the File Manager (File, File Manager), and use
   the Navigator to locate the directory you want to
   back up.

2. Choose Search, Advanced Find. The Advanced Find
   dialog box appears. Specify the range of dates you
   want to copy by typing last week's date in the From
   text box but leaving the To text box empty.

3. Choose Find, and WordPerfect displays a list of all
   files created during the dates you specified.

4. Choose Edit, Select All (Ctrl+S) to select all the files in
   the list; then press Ctrl+C (or choose File, Copy) to
   copy them to a floppy drive.

If WordPerfect runs out of space on the target floppy disk,
it prompts you to insert another, then continues until all
the specified files are safely copied.

Secure your files by using a password

If you have certain files that only your eyes should see, you can protect them by adding a password. Then, you (or anyone else) cannot open or view such files without providing the password.

To add a password to a file, choose File, Password. In the Password dialog box, type the password twice. You won't see the password on-screen as you type it (for security reasons). For this reason, WordPerfect has you enter it twice to make sure you get it right. Finally, the file is not protected until you save it, so be sure to save it before closing the document.

Caution: Don't forget the password! WordPerfect Corporation cannot supply the password for you. Some third-party vendors claim to have programs that can rescue your password-protected files, but these programs involve cost, time, and the chance that they'll fail. One way to make sure you don't forget your password is to use the same password for all your protected files. However, don't write the password on a sticky note and affix it to your computer!

Also, be aware that adding a password to a file does not protect it from being deleted from your hard disk.

If you decide you don't need password protection anymore, open the file, choose File, Password and select **Remove**. Be sure to save the file; if you don't, the password removal does not take effect.

18

CHAPTER

Using Graphics and Lines

Entire books have been written about WordPerfect's graphics features, including integrating text and graphics in desktop publishing enterprises. This chapter doesn't attempt to show you everything you can do with graphics in all situations, but focuses instead on a number of procedures and ideas that you might find helpful in everyday use.

Use the right mouse button to quickly get a graphics menu

Normally when you want to edit a figure box, you select Graphics, Figure, Edit and indicate the figure box with which you want to work. The same is true with other types of graphics elements. You also perform an equivalent number of steps to change the position of or add a caption to a graphics box.

A much quicker way to get the essential menu items for a specific graphics element is to position the mouse pointer over the graphics element you want to edit and click the right mouse button. An abbreviated graphics menu appears. If you selected a figure box, for example, you now can go directly to the Figure Editor, to the Box Position and Size dialog box, or to the Caption Editor for the figure you selected.

Double-click to edit a graphic element

Instead of using the menus, you can enter directly into the editor for any graphic element by double-clicking that element with the mouse. For example, to edit a figure box in the Figure Editor, double-click that figure box.

Don't always wrap text

By default, WordPerfect wraps text around your graphics objects to provide a flowing effect and to avoid mixing text and graphics. At times, however, you want to superimpose text and graphics, in a poster or flyer, for example (see fig. 18.1).

Fig. 18.1 *A graphic object with superimposed text.*

To mix text with a graphic object, move the mouse pointer over the graphics object until the pointer changes to an arrow. Click the secondary (right) mouse button to get an editing menu. Select Box Position, and WordPerfect displays the Box Position and Size dialog box. Deselect the Wrap Text Around Box check box. You now can position the graphic object on top of any of your text or even on any other graphics object.

When Wrap Text Around Box has been disabled, you are not allowed to select the box by clicking it. You must first press the secondary right mouse button, and then choose Select Box from the menu.

Note: If two or more graphics elements are positioned on top of each other, only one of them can be selected and manipulated with the mouse. The others must be selected and changed using menus and dialog boxes.

Know how the different graphics box types compare

WordPerfect has several types of graphics boxes, but once you learn how to deal with one graphics box type, you know how to deal with them all. You can anchor or position any type of graphic anywhere in the document. You also can size any graphics box any way you want. All graphics boxes include options for box lines, outside and inside spacing, caption position, and shading.

The differences among the graphics boxes are the following:

- Some types use the figure editor (figure), some the text editor (text, table), one uses the equation editor (equation), and one can use any of the three editors (user).

- Each type has default lines and shading, but you can change any of them to be like any of the others. Select Graphics, the graphics box type, and Options.

- Each type has a default size and position. For example, figure boxes are 3.25" square, are anchored to the page, and appear at the right margin. Equations boxes stretch from left to right margins and are only tall enough to accommodate the equation within them.

- Each type uses a different numbering sequence and format for captions. Lists that include graphics boxes use the same numbering sequence as the boxes.

- Each type has a default distance between the edge of the graphics box and the outside text, and another between the edge of the box and the contents of that box. You can change these defaults.

Use graphic lines to help text flow

Graphic lines are easy to create and are much more versatile than regular underlines. Use horizontal lines to help separate sections of text (for example, the introductory part of a memo and the text body of a memo). Use vertical lines to help guide the reader (for example, between newspaper style columns).

You can adjust the thickness of a graphic line by clicking the line and then dragging the top or bottom sizing handles. You can change other attributes by double-clicking the line to open an edit dialog box.

Use horizontal graphic lines for signature lines

If you ever have tried to create signature lines using underlining, you know just how hard it is to make them exactly the right length and properly lined up. Using graphic lines can be much easier.

Suppose you want two signature lines, each three inches long, one at the left side and one at the right side. First, position the insertion point on the line of your text where you want the signature lines, and follow these steps:

1. Select Graphics, Line, Horizontal (Ctrl+F11).

2. Select Horizontal Position, Left, and set Length to 3". Choose OK.

3. Again, on the same line, select Graphics, Line, Horizontal (Ctrl+F11).

4. Select Horizontal Position, Right, and set Length to 3". Choose OK.

You now have two perfect 3" signature lines.

Adjust horizontal lines to fit with the rest of your text

If you create a horizontal line by itself on one line of your document, often the text above and beneath the line squeezes together (see fig. 18.2). This quality can become a problem if, for example, you use line numbering because the line numbers also overlap. To make a graphic line occupy the same vertical space as a regular line of text, press the space bar after you create the horizontal line. The line that the graphic line is on expands as if the line had text.

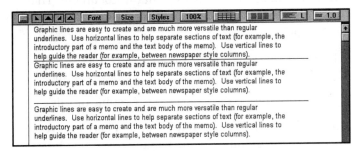

Fig. 18.2 *Two lines, the second of which is followed by a space character.*

Rotate text in a text box

If your printer can print both landscape and portrait on the same page (for example, the HP LaserJet III can do this), you can print rotated text boxes.

Create a text box. Type the text you want in the box, then select **Rotate**, and the increment you want (90, 180, or 270) before you close the Text Box editor.

Note: Although the text may appear rotated in Print Preview, if your printer cannot print both orientations of text on the same page, what you see will *not* print, no matter how hard you try.

Use Graphic on Disk to conserve disk space

Graphic images, especially bit-mapped graphics, take up a lot of disk space. If you use a graphic image as part of a letterhead or logo for your memos, you save another copy of the graphic image each time you save a memo.

To help conserve disk space, when you create a graphic box that you use frequently, tell WordPerfect not to save the graphic, but to use a specified graphic on your disk each time you retrieve, edit, or print the document. That way, you need only one copy of the graphic file. Follow these steps:

1. Select **Graphic, Figure, Create** to go directly to the Figure Editor without first selecting the graphic.

2. In the Figure Editor, select **File, Graphic on Disk.**

3. Click the Retrieve button (or select **File, Retrieve**) to select the graphic file you want to use.

4. Make any changes you want to the graphic, then choose **Close.**

Now when you save the file, it saves only the text, along with references to the graphic file. In one file alone, this feature can save some 1500 bytes of space. On many hard disks, each file occupies a minimum of 4000 bytes. Over time, if you don't use the Graphic on Disk option, you could waste literally megabytes of disk space.

Caution: If you share the file with someone else and she doesn't have access to the same graphics file on her disk, the figure box will print, but the graphic in that box won't. To make sure the graphics prints on another computer, send the graphic file along with your document.

Print white text on a black background

Many printers can print white text on a black background (for example, the HP LaserJet III). To use this feature, follow these steps:

1. Select Graphics, Text Box, Options. Change the Border Styles to None on the top and bottom, and change the Gray Shading to 100%. Choose OK.

2. Select Graphics, Text Box, Create (Alt+F11).

3. Select the text font you want to use (F9) if different from the body of your text. (Bold fonts tend to work better for white text on a black background.)

4. Select Font, Color, and from the Select Text Color dialog box, choose White from the Predefined Colors pop-up menu. Choose OK.

5. Type and edit your text as you normally do. The text in the editing screen appears black, but the font on the status line displays in white. When you are finished, Close the Text Editor.

6. Position and size the text box as you do any other graphics box.

To see the results of your creation, press Print Preview (Shift+F5). However, the acid test comes when you try to print it. If your printer does not support white text on black, you get just a plain black box.

Create drop shadow borders on your graphics boxes

You can change the border styles on any of your graphics boxes, even equation boxes. Position the insertion point *before* the graphics box to which you want to add a drop shadow border, and follow these steps:

1. Select Graphics, the type of graphics box, **Options**. WordPerfect displays the Options dialog box for whatever graphics box type you are setting up.

2. Change the Border Styles so that any two adjoining sides have **Single** lines, and the other two have **Thick** lines. For example, if you want the shadow to drop to the left, select Thick for the Left and Bottom.

3. Make any other options changes and choose OK.

Your graphics box now has lovely drop shadows (see fig. 18.3).

Fig. 18.3   *A figure box with drop shadows.*

Put frequently used graphics in a style

If you often find yourself using the same graphic, in the same type of graphics box, consider placing the graphic in a style. Then when you need the graphic, use that style.

Create a flyer with a full-page border

You can create attractive flyers quickly and easily by using Border Options, a full-page text box, and a large type font. Follow these steps:

1. Select **Graphics, Text Box, Options,** and set the Border Styles the way you want them (for example, drop shadows). You probably also want to change **Gray Shading** to 0%. Choose **OK.**

2. Select **Graphics, Text Box, Create.**

3. Click the **Box Position** button. Set the **Vertical Position** to **Full Page,** the **Horizontal Position** to **Margin, Full,** and deselect the **Wrap Text Around Box.** Choose **OK.**

4. Select **Layout, Justification, Center** (Ctrl+J).

5. Select the fonts you want, and type the text you need. When you are finished, choose **Close.**

Because you deselected the Wrap Text Around Box option, you can add other graphics figure boxes on the same page. You now have a drop shadow box surrounding the entire body of your text (see fig. 18.4). You may have to experiment with fonts, font size, and vertical spacing (use extra hard returns or Advance codes to move the text down).

Use empty figure boxes as check boxes

A simple way to create check boxes (for example, in an application form), is to create small, empty figure boxes and anchor them to a character. A 1/8" by 1/8" box is a good size to begin with. Follow these steps:

1. Select **Graphics, Figure, Create.**

2. In the Figure Editor, click the **Fig Pos** button or select **File, Box Position.**

3. Set the **Anchor Type** to **Character.**

4. Set Both **Width** and **Height** to 1/8" (.125").

5. Choose **OK,** and **Close** the Figure Editor.

6. Add a tab or indent after the box and you have a check box that matches in size approximately one line of text (see fig. 18.5).

Fig. 18.4   *A flyer, using a full-page text box and border options.*

If you want to add drop shadows to a check box, you need to make the box a bit larger (for example, 1/4") because the thick line is too thick for a very small box. Position the insertion point before the Figure Box code and select Graphics, Figure, Options and change the Border Styles.

The WordPerfect Character set does include two check box characters, but both are a bit too small for most check box needs.

If you create a check box you like, include it in a style or a macro.

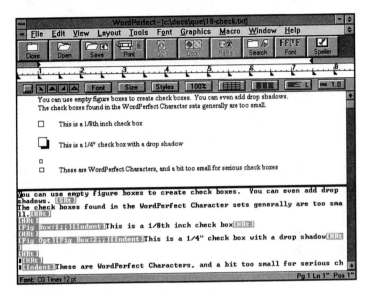

Fig. 18.5 *Using empty figure boxes for check boxes.*

Create equations in the body of the text with the **INLINE** macro

When you want to create an equation as part of the body of your text, you may find it difficult to set things up properly. Fortunately, WordPerfect comes with a special macro just for you.

When you Play (Alt+F10) the INLINE macro, WordPerfect creates an equation box, anchored to a character, that takes up just the amount of space needed for the equation and places it right at the insertion point (see fig. 18.6).

Match equation text to your text font

WordPerfect equations print in one of three different type styles: Courier, Times Roman, or Helvetica. Regardless of the printer or type styles you have, WordPerfect matches its equations the best it can with your fonts. For example, if your document uses Prestige Elite, the equation uses Times Roman, even on a dot-matrix printer.

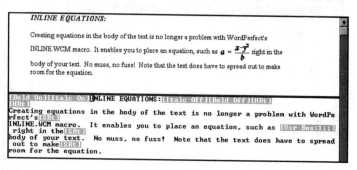

Fig. 18.6 *An INLINE equation box.*

To assure that your equation's type style matches that of your document, do one of the following:

1. Set your document's Initial Font by selecting Layout, Document, Initial Font. This method is recommended because it also enables matching page numbers, footnotes, headers, and footers.

2. Place an Equation Box options code immediately preceding the Equation Box code. You need not make any changes to the options, but the placement of the code tells WordPerfect to match the equation font with the current text font.

Create attention-grabbing pull quotes

Pull quotes, quotations lifted from the body of your text, can add interest to your documents because they get the reader's attention. To create a pull-quote macro, follow these steps:

1. Select the text you want to use in the quote.

2. Press Macro Record (Ctrl+F10) and name this macro something you can remember, such as PULL. Choose **Record**.

3. Select Edit, Copy (Ctrl+Insert).

4. Press Select (F8).

5. Select **Graphics**, Text **B**ox, **C**reate.

6. Press Ctrl+S, **L**arge (or select **F**ont, **S**ize, **L**arge). You could add other attributes as well, such as bold and italics.

7. Select Edit, **P**aste (Shift+Insert).

8. Choose **C**lose.

9. Stop the macro by selecting **M**acro, **S**top (Ctrl+Shift+F10).

Now you can use the mouse to position your pull-quote box wherever you want it, for example, between two columns of text (see fig. 18.7). You also can double-click the text box and further edit the text.

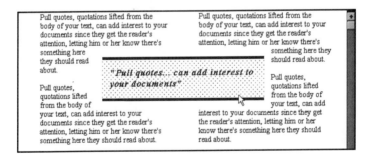

Fig. 18.7 *A pull quote between two columns.*

To use the macro again, select the text you want to appear in the pull quote, then press Macro Play (Alt+F10), and enter **PULL**.

19

Commenting, Importing, and Exporting

Sometimes text creation is a collaborative effort. You may write one part of a report while someone else prepares the data tables. WordPerfect offers several special tools for those working together in creating a joint-effort document.

Attach comments to your documents

WordPerfect's Comment feature lets you leave notes for a colleague in a WordPerfect document. Position the insertion point wherever you want to leave a comment and select Tools, Comment, Create. In the text box, type the text of your comment. Notice that you can use bold, underline, and italics for emphasis. To place a hard return in your comment, you must press Ctrl+Enter. When you are done, select **OK** and a comment appears across the page (see fig. 19.1). The comment does not print, but instead acts like a sticky note to yourself or to your collaborator.

Note: A comment can contain roughly 1000 characters. WordPerfect stops accepting characters when the limit is reached.

Add comments to your text. These non-printing comments can include **bold** or _underlines_ or even *italics*

Fig. 19.1 *An example of a comment.*

If you want to add to or edit a comment, double-click the comment to display the Edit Comment dialog box.

If you receive a file from someone else that contains comments, select Edit, **Search** (F2), **Codes**, Comment, and press Enter to quickly locate any comments scattered throughout your document.

Caution: Comments may not convert to another word processing format. If you're not sure, try a test document to see whether the comments pass from one word processing format back to WordPerfect.

Store text in non-printing comments

You also can convert small blocks of text into non-printing comments. Suppose you have a paragraph in a standard form letter that you use only occasionally. You could keep the paragraph in a comment and use it only when needed.

To convert text to a comment, select the text and then choose Tools, Comment, Create. WordPerfect automatically places the selected text into a comment box. WordPerfect will not create the Comment if the text you select exceeds the limit for comments.

To convert a comment box back to text, position the insertion point somewhere *after* the comment box and select Tools, Comment, Convert to Text. The contents of the comment box become a printable part of your document.

Work with non-WordPerfect documents

WordPerfect converts over 40 different word processing formats. To add another non-WordPerfect document to your own, select File, **R**etrieve, and answer Yes. Word-Perfect guesses what format was used for the file and displays that format's name in the Convert File Format dialog box. If the suggested format is not correct, use the list box to find and select the one you want. Select **OK** to retrieve the file, or Cancel to stop the procedure.

Don't expect special formatting to convert

Although WordPerfect can convert other formats into WordPerfect, some features of the other word processing program probably won't remain intact after the conversion. Certain features don't exist in both programs, or features can work very differently in the two programs.

If you plan to work with others who use non-WordPerfect word processors, decide which of your programs will produce the final output. The rest of the collaborators are better off creating relatively generic text (including bold, italics, and tabs), leaving all of the special formatting to the person using the final format program.

Make sure you save the conversion

If you open a non-WordPerfect file directly instead of retrieving it, you also convert it to the WordPerfect format.

If, after making changes or additions, you save the document, WordPerfect saves the file in the same format it was in before you opened it. To keep the newly edited document in the WordPerfect format, select WP5.1/5.2 from the Format list box in the Save As dialog box.

If you want to keep the original file as well as your corrections, supply a new name for the file you are about to save. Until you save the document as a WP file, WordPerfect continues to force you to use the Save As dialog box, even when you select File, Save.

Use intermediate formats if no direct conversion exists

If you can't directly convert a document from the other person's word processing program to yours, you may be able to work around this problem by finding an intermediate format that both of you can use. For example, the RTF (Rich Text Format) is a fairly common generic word processing format that many word processing programs understand. Another such format is the IBM DCA format. Of course, you also can use the generic ASCII format, but you lose nearly every formatting code in the process.

Squeeze an entire spreadsheet into your document

Getting spreadsheet data into a WordPerfect document is as easy as 1-2-3. Retrieve (File, Retrieve) any Lotus or Lotus-compatible spreadsheet (for example, PlanPerfect, Excel, or Quattro Pro), and WordPerfect places the spreadsheet in a table.

If the spreadsheet is too large to fit in your document, try the following:

- Reduce the font size, and stay with a fixed pitch font (for example, Line Printer). Remember to return to your document font following the spreadsheet table.

- Reduce the margins.

- Eliminate unneeded rows or columns of the table.

- Place the spreadsheet on a separate page and select landscape page orientation.

If none of these methods work, rethink what it is you really need or want. Perhaps you only need a portion of the spreadsheet.

Import only portions of a spreadsheet

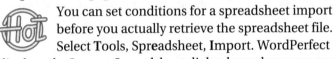 You can set conditions for a spreadsheet import before you actually retrieve the spreadsheet file. Select Tools, Spreadsheet, Import. WordPerfect displays the Import Spreadsheet dialog box where you can specify the name of the file and the specific range of cells you want to import.

You also can import named ranges. Ask the person creating the spreadsheet to name ranges of cells that apply to the document you both are working on. Then in the Import Spreadsheet dialog box, click the Range Name text box, and WordPerfect displays any named ranges in the spreadsheet. Select the one you want and choose OK.

Use spreadsheet links if you plan to update your data

If the spreadsheet you want to import is frequently updated, and if your document is used more than once, create a spreadsheet link (Tools, Spreadsheet, Create Link). Linking means that when data changes in the spreadsheet, the information is passed along to your document.

The dialog box for creating a link is the same as for a normal spreadsheet import. You can link your document to the entire spreadsheet or to specific and named ranges.

Document to Spreadsheet links are updated only when you open a document with a spreadsheet link in it. However, even then WordPerfect updates the spreadsheet only if you choose that option (Tools, Spreadsheet, Link options, Update Links on Document Open).

Understand which OLE data links to use

OLE (pronounced O-lay), which stands for Object Linking and Embedding, enables various Windows applications to exchange data and maintain links for updating that data. WordPerfect is an OLE *client*, which means that it can only link to files or objects created by other Windows applications that are *servers*.

Linking means that WordPerfect maintains contact with another server-created file. Embedding means that WordPerfect places a copy of the object in its own file, remembering what program was used to create it.

If you want quick access to the source application, but don't need to work with the source file by itself, use Object Embedding. However, if you need to use the source file by itself (for example, a spreadsheet or graph) outside of WordPerfect, then use Object Linking. If you work on a network where others may use or update the source file, also use Object Linking.

Find out quickly what applications are OLE servers

To determine quickly which programs can be OLE servers, select Edit, Insert Object. The Insert Object dialog box lists those applications that have reported to Windows as OLE servers. If the application you hoped would work is not listed, you may be able to use DDE links, or transfer data using the Windows Clipboard.

Don't forget the Windows Clipboard

The Windows Clipboard provides a handy method of getting data or graphics from one application to another. Special formatting (in the case of text) is lost when moving between two different applications, but remains intact when moving between WordPerfect files. Graphics are reduced to bitmaps.

Index

hidden codes
   deleting, 52
   moving with text, 34-35
Hide Button Bar (Button Bar
   QuickMenu) command, 47
hiding Button Bars and Ruler, 15-16
high resolution graphics, 108
horizontal graphics lines, 188-189
hyphenation
   dictionary, customizing, 13
   text in columns, 82-83
hyphens, replacing dashes, 144

I

icons
   Tables, 112
   WordPerfect for Windows, 9
Import Spreadsheet dialog box, 203
importing data, spreadsheet,
   202-203
Include Subdocument dialog box,
   146
indents, 18-20
indexes, 142-143
Init Font button, 91-92
INLINE macro, 40, 195
INSERT macro, 40
Insert Object dialog box, 204
insertion points, 6-7, 29
installing WordPerfect for Windows,
   4
interfaces, Common User Access,
   7-8
invoices, 170
Italic attribute, 20-21

J-K

Justification (Layout menu)
   command, 64
JUSTIFY macro, 40
justifying text, 64

kerning, 98-99
keyboards, 166-167
   Common User Access, 162
      Ctrl+key combinations, 39
   cursor movement, 28-29
   files, 4
   macros, compiling, 167
   mouse, 4-5
   selecting text, 32-33

keys, 7-8
keystrokes, Common User Access,
   7-8
   see also shortcut keys

L

labels, 73-77, 170
LABELS macro, 40, 72-73
Language (Tools menu) command,
   128
Language dialog box, 128
languages, Macro Dialog, 162
laser labels, 72
leading, 98
length of columns, 81-82
Letter spacing, 98
letters, 170
libraries, style, 87
Line (Graphics menu) command,
   188
Line (Layout menu) command, 56,
   59, 63, 82-83
LINENUM macro, 40
lines
   graphic, 188-189
   signature, 188-189
linking spreadsheets, 203-204
list boxes, 5
lists
   merging to tables, 121-123
   numbering, 150
   sorting, 143-144
Location of Files dialog box, 71
locking table cells, 118
Lotus 1-2-3-compatible documents,
   202

M

macro buttons, text, 50
Macro Command Inserter dialog
   box, 166
Macro Dialog commands, 162-164
Macro Dialog language, 162
Macro Help, 157-158
Macro Manual, 162
macros
   adding to menus, 160-161
   assigning to Button Bar, 49-50
   compiling, 167
   Ctrl-key combinations, 38-39
   files, 4

outlines, paragraph numbering, 151
pausing, 159-160
predefined, 39-41
    assigning Ctrl+key name, 41-42
    recording, 37-38
    shortcut names, 162-163
    ShowMe!, 159
    temporary, 164-165
    writing, 158
        Macro Command Inserter, 166
Macros Manual, 157-158
mailing labels, 73, 170
Manual Kerning dialog box, 99
margin markers for columns, 82
Mark (Tools menu) command, 137, 140-141
Mark Cross-Reference dialog box, 140
MARK macro, 41
Master Document (Tools menu) command, 146
mathematics in tables, 156
measurements, Ruler, 53
MEMO macro, 41
memory requirements, printing graphics, 110
memos, Merge command, 173
menus, 16
    adding macros, 160-161
    Application Control, 9
Merge (Tools menu) command, 169-171
    memos, 173-174
merges, 170-173
merging lists to tables, 121-123
minimizing
    programs, 129
    WordPerfect for Windows, 9
modes
    Draft, 17
    Select, 32
Mor-Proof spell checker, Grammatik, 131
mouse, 5-6
    accessing graphics menu, 185-186
    double-clicking, 6
    Drag and Drop, 34
    files, copying and moving, 178

keyboards, 4-5
moving in tables, 114
opening Reveal Codes window, 27-28
selecting
    cells, columns, rows, or tables, 115
    text, 32-33
Move/Rename (File menu) command, 178
Move/Rename File dialog box, 163
moving
    files, 177-178
    insertion point with keystrokes, 29
    outlines, 152-153
    tabs with Ruler, 62-63
    text, 34-35
multiple copies, files, printing, 108
Multiple Pages dialog box, 106-107

N

name-tag labels, 73, 170
names of fields, 170
Navigator, File Manager, 176-177
newsletters, text in columns, 81-82
newspaper-style columns, tables, 118
non-printing
    codes, 103
    comments, 200-201
non-WordPerfect documents, 201-202
numbering
    footnotes and endnotes, 145
    lists, 150
    pages, 134-143
numbering styles, outlines, 154
numbers, inserting in paragraphs, 151

O

Object Linking and Embedding (OLE), 204
odd pages, printing, 107
opening
    files, 16-17
    windows, Reveal Codes, 27-28
Options (Button Bar QuickMenu) command, 47
Options menu commands, Move/Rename, 163

flow with graphic lines, 188
flush right, 18
fonts, matching equation text,
195-196
formatting with styles, 84-85
hyphenation, 82-83
justifying, 64
macro buttons, 50
moving, 34-35
newsletters, 81-82
pasting, 8, 33
printing
quality, 108
white on black background,
191
replacing, 31
restoring deleted, 31
rotating in text boxes, 189-190
selecting, 33-36
storing in non-printing
comments, 200-201
tabular, turning into tables,
113-114
viewing full width, 17-18
wrapping around graphics,
186-187
Text Box (Graphics menu)
command, 191-193, 197
Text Box editor, 190
Thesaurus, 4, 129-130
files, 13
Thesaurus (Tools menu) command,
130
tickets, creating with labels, 79
tractor feed labels, *see* dot-matrix
labels
TRANSPOS macro, 41
TrueType fonts, 90
tutorial files, 4
two-word names, 144
typefaces, 94-95
Typesetting (Layout menu)
command, 66, 98
Typesetting dialog box, 66, 98
typographic symbols, 22

U

Undelete (Edit menu) command, 31
Underline attribute, 20-21
underlining, fill-in-the-blank forms,
65-66
Undo (Edit menu) command, 53-54,
116

updating
files, 180
QuickFinder File Indexer,
181-182
Using Macros (Help menu)
command, 40, 158

V

versions, WordPerfect for Windows,
12
videocassette labels, 73
viewing text, 17-18
views, 102

W-Z

white text, printing on black
background, 191
width of columns, 82
wild cards, Speller, 129-130
WIN.INI files, editing, 11
Windows
calculator, adding to
WordPerfect, 160
Clipboard, 205
windows, Reveal Codes, opening,
27-28
Windows Program Manager, *see*
Program Manager
word spacing, 98
WordPerfect Characters dialog box,
22-23
WordPerfect for DOS, 13, 105
WordPerfect for Windows
adding Windows calculator, 160
installing, 4
Macros Manual, 157-158
minimizing, 9
printer drivers, 105-106
speeding up, 10
WordPerfect Units, 53
WP Characters (Font menu)
command, 22
WP File Navigator (View menu)
command, 176
wrapping text around graphics,
186-187
writing macros, 158, 166
writing styles, Grammatik, 131

Zoom, 17-18
Zoom (View menu) command, 18
Zoom feature, 102-103